Girl's guide to sewing

Girl's guide to sewing

Cheryl Owen

NEW HOLLAND

First published in 2014 by
New Holland Publishers
London • Sydney • Cape Town • Auckland
www.newhollandpublishers.com • www.newholland.com.au

The Chandlery Unit 114 50 Westminster Bridge Road London SE1 7QY UK
1/66 Gibbes Street Chatswood NSW 2067 Australia
Wembley Square First Floor Solan Road Gardens Cape Town 8001 South Africa
218 Lake Road Northcote Auckland New Zealand

A catalogue record of this book is available at the British Library and at the National Library
of Australia

ISBN: 9781780094779

10 9 8 7 6 5 4 3 2 1

Publisher: Fiona Schultz
Editor: Simona Hill
Designer: Tracy Loughlin
Stylist: Sue Stubbs
Photographer: Sue Stubbs
Production director: Olga Dementiev
Printer: Toppan Leefung Printing Limited

Follow New Holland Publishers on
Facebook: www.facebook.com/NewHollandPublishers

Contents

INTRODUCTION

It is wonderful to be able to sew your own clothes and to make accessories. Not only does it save you heaps of money but you will also have something unique and to your own specifications. Whether you are new to sewing or already accomplished, this book will show you all you need to know to create glorious clothing, fashion accessories and soft furnishings. None of the projects will take more than a day to make and there are also ideas on how to upcycle items that you already have.

All of the projects would make lovely gifts; handcrafted presents are always special — if you can bear to part with them! There is a choice of cases to make to protect today's gadgetry. Most of the items use small amounts of fabric, which gives you the chance to embark on that fabulous stash of fabric you already own or to choose new ones economically. If you are an accomplished dress-maker, take the projects further and use them as inspiration to create your own designs.

Techniques

EQUIPMENT

You will probably have a basic sewing kit even if you are new to sewing. Keep all the items together and use them on fabric and trimming only, otherwise they could become dirty and cutting tools blunt. Work on a clean, flat surface with good lighting, a daylight-simulation bulb is kind to the eye and doesn't distort the colour of fabrics and threads. Take care to keep sharp tools and glues beyond the reach of young children and pets.

Pattern-making paper

You will need large sheets of paper to make patterns for clothes. Haberdashery stores and departments stock pattern-making paper which is at least 91 cm (36 in) wide. Traditional spot and cross pattern paper is printed with a grid of spots and crosses that you can use as a guide for drawing accurate right angles and straight lines, they are placed at 2 cm (¾ in) or 2.5 cm (1 in) intervals. Alternatively, use parcel paper, which also comes in large sizes. If you have to fold your patterns to store them, press flat with a dry iron before you use them. Tracing paper or baking paper is very useful if you need to see through the pattern, for example when positioning motifs. Small patterns can be made from most papers that you have to hand, but don't use newspaper as it will dirty your hands and fabric.

Pattern-making tools

Draw patterns accurately with a mechanical pencil or fine pen. If you use an ordinary pencil such as an HB leaded pencil, keep it sharpened to a point. Draw straight lines against a ruler and circles with a pair of compasses. Use a set square for accurate angles.

Measuring tools

A plastic-coated or cloth tape measure is indispensable for measuring curves, fabric quantities and of course, measuring yourself! A transparent 30 cm (12 in) rule is a handy size for measuring and drawing against. Although not vital, if you plan to sew a lot of clothes and home furnishings, a metre (yard) stick is useful for measuring long lengths and making clothes patterns. A 15 cm (6 in) sewing gauge has a slider that can be set at different widths for marking hems and sewing, there may be one among the accessories of your sewing machine.

Scissors

Cut paper with paper scissors. Bent-handled dressmaking shears are the most accurate and comfortable to cut fabric with, the angle of the lower blade allows the fabric to lie flat. Shears are available in different sizes, always test before buying, because they need to feel comfortable in your hand. Top-quality shears are expensive but if cared for they will last a lifetime. Small, sharp embroidery scissors are vital for clipping seam allowances and threads. Pinking shears cut a zig-zag fray-resistant edge for neatening seams and can be used to cut fabric that is prone to fraying. Keep scissors in a cloth case when not in use.

Fabric markers

Marks made with an air-erasable pen will gradually fade away and those made with a water-soluble pen can be removed with water. Traditional tailor's chalk is available in a few colours in wedge form or as a pencil, the marks will brush off but a slight residue will remain. Always test fabric markers on scrap fabric first. A fine, sharp pencil can be used on fabric but the marks will stay.

NEEDLES

Sewing machine needles

Needles for sewing machines come in a range of sizes with different-shaped points, the lower the number the finer the point. Universal needles sized 70–90 (9–14) are the most regularly used. Use a sharp-point needle on woven fabrics and stitch non-woven fabrics such as jersey with a ball-point needle. It is important to replace sewing machine needles often, as they soon become blunt and put strain on your sewing machine.

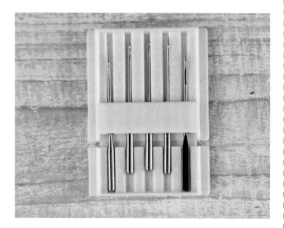

Hand sewing needles

In this case, the higher the number the shorter and finer the needle. Sharps needles are long, general purpose needles, use them to tack (baste), slipstitch and sew on buttons. Crewel embroidery needles have a large eye to accommodate embroidery thread. Beading needles come in very long or short lengths, they are particularly fine so that they can slide through small beads.

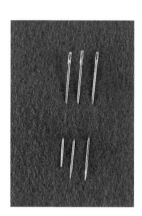

Pins

Dressmaking pins come in different thicknesses, household pins are the most commonly used. Lace and bridal pins are slender and will not mark delicate fabrics. Coloured glass-headed pins show up well on a large expanse of fabric.

Bodkin

This needle-like tool has a large eye and blunt tip. Fasten a bodkin to a drawstring to draw it through a channel or to the end of a fabric tube to turn it right side out. If you do not have a bodkin, a safety pin will suffice.

Rouleau turner

Also called a tube turner, a rouleau turner has a latch hook at one end. To use, slip the rouleau turner through a fabric tube, hook the latch hook onto the end of the fabric then draw the rouleau turner back through the tube to turn it right side out. A safety pin can be used instead but it will be a slower process.

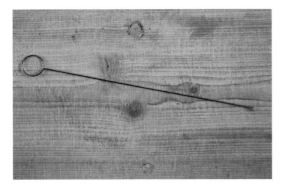

Bias binding maker

This neat gadget comes in different sizes to make different widths of bias binding. Draw a bias-cut strip of fabric through the bias-binding maker to turn under the fabric edges, then press in place to form a binding.

SEWING MACHINE

There will always be a place for hand sewing but stitching by machine saves time and gives a professional finish. The sewing machine is a major investment so don't rush into buying. Ask friends and family for recommendations. Choose a reputable dealer and test run a few machines using different fabrics to make comparisons in order to see which you prefer. The machine should be simple to thread and the speed easy to control. A machine that does straight stitch, zig-zag stitch and neat buttonholes will cover most peoples' needs but you may also consider the sophisticated models that are now available and offer machine embroidery and computerised controls.

How it works

Despite the large range, all sewing machines are fairly similar to operate. Read the manual to familiarise yourself with the machine's features and operations. Basically, the presser foot holds the fabric in place, while the needle threaded with the upper thread penetrates the fabric and goes into the bobbin area below to pick up the lower thread in order to make a stitch. This particular machine (opposite) has a lift-up lid that conceals the spool holder that holds the reel of the upper thread, the bobbin winder, foot pressure dial and the thread tension dial. This is a practical design feature as the lid protects these machine parts from getting dusty.

Thread tension dial

This dial regulates the tension between the upper and lower thread to form flat, even stitches. The stitches will pucker if the tension is too tight but if it is too loose, the stitches will be slack and won't be able to hold the fabric layers together.

Stitch length dial

The numbers on the dial represent either the length of the stitch in millimetres or the number of stitches per inch.

Stitch width dial

Set this dial at 0 for straight stitch or adjust it for the width of a zig-zag stitch.

Reverse stitch lever

Lift the reverse stitch lever to stitch backwards. Reverse stitch for about 8 mm (5/16 in) at the start and finish of a seam to stop the ends of the seam unravelling or to reinforce the start of the seam, for instance at the top of a pocket.

Needle plate

This metal plate covers the area under the presser foot. The needle enters a slot in the centre of the plate to grab the bobbin thread concealed below. There will be a series of lines on the needle plate to use as seam width guides.

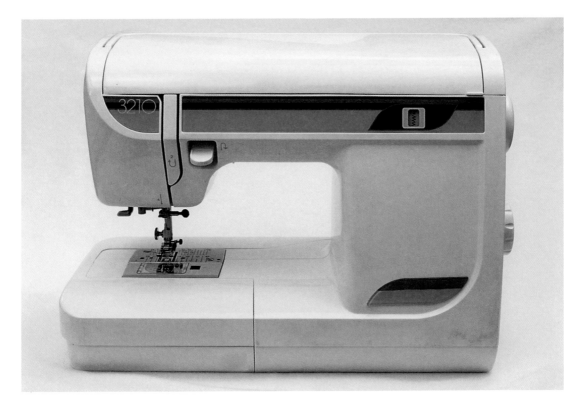

Bobbins

Small metal and plastic spools called bobbins are wound with the lower thread and housed underneath the stitching area. When the bobbin thread runs out, it can be refilled by winding on the bobbin winder.

Power supply

Check that the electrical voltage of the machine is the same as your power supply. For safety, keep the power supply switched off and unplugged when setting up the machine and when not in use. Plug in the cord socket then insert the plug into the power supply and switch on the power.

Sewing light

Always work in good light. The sewing light on the machine will keep the stitching area well lit and is especially useful when stitching dark colours.

Foot control

Stitch with the foot control on a flat floor surface. The harder the foot control is pressed, the faster the machine will run. The sewing speed can be varied on most machines.

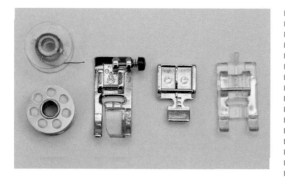

Above: Bobbins and presser feet.

Hand wheel

Once the machine is threaded, and the stitch set to the required length, lift the presser foot and turn the hand wheel to raise the needle. Slip your fabric under the needle then turn the hand wheel to lower the needle until it just touches the fabric. Now lower the presser foot to begin stitching.

PRESSER FEET

The machine will have a standard presser foot and probably a few specialist presser feet too. There is a level to lift the presser foot up and down. The feet can be changed by snapping them on and off or unscrewing and screwing back on again.

Standard foot

This will be the most often used foot. Use for straight and zig-zag stitch.

Zipper foot

Use to stitch beside a raised edge such as a zip.

Piping foot

Use to stitch a raised trimming such as piping or a pom pom trim. If you do not have a piping foot, use a zipper foot instead.

Buttonhole foot

Use to work buttonholes.

Overlock foot

Use for zig-zag stitching or you can use a standard foot instead.

Blind hem foot

Use for making invisible hems, the foot ensures that the needle catches only one or two threads.

MATERIALS

Much of the fun of sewing, is choosing the materials that you want to use. Most of the fabrics in this book are made from natural fibres such as cotton and linen, which are easy to sew and ideal for beginners. Fabrics made from natural fibres are prone to shrink so it is best to wash them before cutting out. Fabric is sold by the metre (yard), meaning that it is measured along its length but as many of these projects use small amounts of fabric, the quantity needed is given as the size of a rectangle or square. This will allow you to delve into the growing stash of fabric that most keen stitchers have accumulated. Allow extra fabric to match stripes and checks or to position designs symmetrically.

Cotton

The range of cotton fabrics is vast. Many patterned cottons are produced with patchwork and quilting in mind and they are complemented by co-ordinating plain coloured cottons. These are often called quilting cottons and have been used for many of the projects in this book. If cotton fabric is listed in the 'You will need' list that accompanies each project, it refers to quilting-weight cotton. Calico (muslin) is a cheap utility fabric; use it to practise sewing techniques or to make slipper soles.

Linen

This strong fabric drapes well although it creases easily. Linen blended with polyester is cheaper to buy, it creases less but the quality is poorer.

Soft furnishing fabric

These fabrics are durable and come in various finishes, patterns and colours. They are usually 137 cm (54 in) wide. Some soft furnishing fabrics have the added bonus of a protective stain-resistant finish.

Interfacing

Stiffen fabric with interfacing to add strength and support. It is available as an iron-on (fusible) or sew-in application and comes in different weights including lightweight, firm flexible and heavyweight. Press the shiny side of iron-on interfacing to the wrong side of the fabric to fuse the layers together. When pressing interfacing, hold the iron in place for a few seconds then lift and place it in another position and continue. Sliding the iron over the interfacing could make it wrinkle. Tack (baste) sew-in interfacing to the wrong side of the fabric around the outer edges.

Iron-on medium-loft fleece

Adds soft structure to the fabric. Press the fabric to the fleece rather than the other way around, as the heat does not penetrate the fleece surface easily. Once applied, don't worry about pressing fabric with fleece added; it will retain its bounce.

Bonding web

This double-sided adhesive web has a paper backing and is used to bond layers of fabric together. Use bonding web to fuse motifs cut from fabric to a background fabric for appliqué work.

Wadding (batting)

Sandwich a layer of wadding between fabrics to pad them. Wadding comes in various weights and is available made from manmade or natural fibres including cotton, wool and eco-friendly bamboo. Bear in mind that wadding made from natural fibres may shrink, whereas those made from polyester won't. Insulated wadding is heat resistant, use it in coasters and place mats.

Bias binding

This practical binding is a strip of bias-cut fabric with the long edges pressed under. Cotton and satin bias binding can be bought in packs or by the metre. They come in a few different widths and colours including patterned fabrics. However, it is economical and more versatile to make your own, see page 29

THREADS
Sewing threads

Choose a strong, durable sewing thread with some flexibility in a colour to match your fabric. Use a general-purpose mercerized cotton thread for woven natural-fibre fabrics. General-purpose polyester thread stretches more than cotton thread; use it on woven synthetics and knitted fabrics. Strong polyester thread is available in a small range of colours for top stitching, making buttonholes and sewing buttons.

Embroidery threads

Stranded cotton embroidery thread is very versatile and is nice to handle. The skeins of thread are inexpensive, come in a wide choice of colours and are made up of six strands that can be separated for fine work. Stranded cotton embroidery thread has been used for the embroidery projects in this book. There are also lots of other threads and yarns available for embroidery that can be embroidered by hand or couched in place with a machine zig-zag stitch or by hand. Machine embroidery threads have a smooth sheen and come in a broad range of colours. Use them for decorative zig-zag stitching.

TRIMMINGS

There is an eclectic choice of trimmings to enhance your sewn creations. Sew pom-pom edgings into a seam using a piping or zipper foot or clip off the individual pom-poms and add them to a finished make. Ribbons come in lots of styles, colours and widths. Ric-rac has an attractive wavy edge, allowing it to be applied to curved shapes as well as used straight. Apply metal studs for an edgy look, they have prongs underneath that are inserted through the fabric and folded under. At the other extreme, use scraps of lace for a shabby chic appeal. Most often used for practical purposes, consider decorating a project with pretty buttons. Cover self-cover buttons with fabric.

Metal eyelets

For a professional finish, attach metal eyelets with a fixing tool, which is supplied in the eyelet pack.

FASTENINGS
Zips (zippers)

For a neat finish, close two edges of fabric with a zip (zipper) fastening. If you are new to sewing, don't be nervous about using zips, they are not that difficult to handle and once mastered, have lots of applications. Stitch zips with a zipper foot on your sewing machine.

Popper fasteners

Make cases easy to open and close with snap fasteners. They come with a fixing tool.

Cotton tape

Make ties and straps from this cheap woven tape. It is widely available and comes in a few widths and colours.

TECHNIQUES

The techniques described here are used not just for the sewing projects in this book but for almost any time you sew too. Always try methods that are new to you on scrap fabric before embarking on a project. When following instructions, it is important to use either metric or imperial measurements but not a combination of the two.

Keep a sewing box to hand containing all your equipment. This should hold dressmaking shears, embroidery scissors, ruler, tape measure, dressmaking pins, sewing threads to match your fabrics, needles, a bodkin, rouleau turner, fabric markers, and paper scissors for cutting paper patterns.

PREPARATION AND CUTTING

Doubtless, you will want to start cutting your fabric as soon as you can but take your time. Cutting out is an important part of the making process and shouldn't be rushed as mistakes can be costly. Remember the saying 'measure twice, cut once' and position patterns accurately and economically. Selvedges (the neatened edges that run the length of the fabric) are often tightly woven, and can make the fabric pucker. Selvedges can be trimmed off before cutting out the fabric pieces to ensure a smooth finish. If the fabric is creased, press it with an iron. Always cut out on a flat surface such as a table or the floor.

Using patterns

There are useful templates and pattern diagrams throughout, although many of the projects in this book are simply made from squares and rectangles that can be drawn directly onto the fabric with a fabric marker, using a set square and rule for accuracy. Sewing patterns have an arrow on them that indicates the grain line. Keep the grain line parallel with the fabric selvedge when positioning the pattern on the fabric.

To cut pairs of patterns, fold the fabric lengthways or widthways to make a double layer. Pin the pattern or draw it on top. Patterns in which the fabric should be cut to the fold have an arrow with the ends turned toward the fold line. Match the fold line to the folded edge of the fabric. Otherwise, keep the fabric single. Cut the fabric along the edge of the pattern or along the outline drawn on the fabric, keep the fabric as flat as possible and don't cut along the fold line. Unpin the pattern and mark any dots or crosses on the fabric with a fabric marker. Save fabric scraps to test the stitches and the heat of the iron.

Positioning motifs

If the fabric has a distinctive motif, you may want to show it off, on the centre of a bag or cushion, for example. Centre stripes and checks so that they will be placed symmetrically when the item is made. Remember that you may need to buy a larger amount of fabric to allow for positioning motifs, stripes and checks.

Make a pattern from tracing or baking paper so that you can see through it. Mark on the grain line and seam lines, this means that if the seam allowance is 1 cm (⅜ in), draw the seam line 1 cm (⅜ in) in from the outer edges. Fold the pattern into quarters to find the centre then open it out flat again. Place the pattern over the motif on the fabric, matching the grain lines and centring the motif. Pin in place and cut out.

Making a circular pattern

Describe small circles on paper with a sharp pencil and a pair of compasses. To make a large circular pattern, for example, for a circular skirt or a round tablecloth, it is simple to make a string and pencil compass to make a quarter circle pattern. Start with a piece of paper that has two adjacent edges that measure at least the radius of the intended circle. Starting at a corner, measure and mark the radius on one edge of the paper. Tie a length of string to a sharp pencil. Fix a map pin up through the first corner of the paper. Hold the pencil upright on the radius mark and tie the other end to the map pin, keeping the string taut. Draw a quarter circle between the two adjacent edges of the paper.

HAND STITCHES
Tacking (basting)

Join fabric layers together temporarily with tacking (basting) stitches before stitching on the sewing machine. If possible, keep the fabric flat on a table for accuracy, lifting it only for sewing shaped areas. Use a contrast coloured sewing thread so the stitches are visible and make straight stitches no longer than 1 cm (⅜ in). Generally, sew just inside the seam line so that the stitches are easy to remove. Sometimes it is necessary to tack (baste) along the seam line for accuracy. Remove the tacking (basting) stitches after stitching unless advised otherwise. You can also tack (baste) by machine, use the longest straight stitch. This is useful for tacking (basting) interfacing or wadding to fabric.

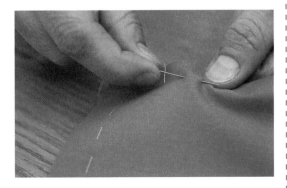

Slipstitch

Join two folded edges together to close a gap or one folded edge to a flat surface to secure a hem or bias binding. Working from right to left with single thread, bring the needle out through one folded edge.

Pick up a few threads of the fabric on the opposite edge and insert the needle back through the folded edge about 6 mm (¼ in) along from where it emerged. Keep the stitches small and repeat along the length.

Herringbone stitch

Work hand-sewn hems with a herringbone stitch. Work the stitches from left to right with the needle pointing to the left. Bring the needle out close to the hem edge, make a small stitch in the fabric above the hem 6 mm (¼ in) to the right, then make a small stitch in the hem the same distance along. Continue to alternate the stitches, spacing them evenly.

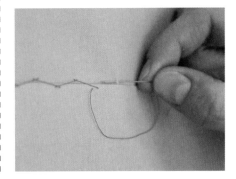

SEAMS

A seam joins two or more layers of fabric together and the seam allowance is the area between the stitching and the raw edge of the fabric. It is important to keep the seam allowance consistent as you stitch a seam so that the fabric pieces match. Align the raw edge of the fabric with the relevant line on the needle plate to keep the seam allowance constant. The seam line is the imaginary line to stitch along.

Common seam allowances are 6 mm (¼ in), 1 cm (⅜ in) and 1.5 cm (⅝ in) and are used throughout the book. Match the seam allowances and raw edges and pin them together. Either insert pins at right angles to the seam line, as this allows you to stitch over them or insert them along the seam line pointing toward the start of the seam and remove then as you stitch. See which method you prefer, it could be a combination of both. If you are new to stitching on a sewing machine or working on an awkward area, tack the layers together first.

Sewing a Flat Seam

1 This is the simplest type of seam and the most often used. With the raw edges level, stitch along the seam line. To turn a corner, stitch to the corner of the seam line and leaving the needle in the fabric, take your foot off the power and lift the presser foot. Pivot the fabric so that the next edge to be stitched is facing you. Lower the presser foot and continue stitching the seam.

2 When joining a curved edge to a straight edge, clip into the straight seam allowance at regular intervals to help the seam allowance lay flat. Pin or tack the seam, then stitch in place.

Layering Seams

Reduce the bulk of fabric in a seam allowance by trimming each fabric by a different amount after the seam has been stitched.

Clipping Corners and Curves

This helps the seam allowances lay flat and reduces the bulk of fabric in the item when it is turned right side out. Use embroidery scissors to cut the seam allowance diagonally across a corner, taking care not to cut the stitching. Clip 'V' shapes into a curved seam allowance, almost to the stitching. The tighter the curve, the closer the clips should be.

Tidying Seams

Use an open zig-zag stitch to tidy the raw edges of seams or stitch a close zig-zag stitch for decoration. Protect raw edges of seams that will be prone to wear with a zig-zag stitch. If stitching a seam on knitted fabric such as jersey, set the machine to a narrow zig-zag stitch or stitch hems on knitted fabric with a wide zig-zag stitch to allow for stretch. Seams can be tidied before or after they are stitched. If you think that you may alter an item, on clothing, for example, zig-zag the seam after it has been stitched. Always test zig-zag stitching on a scrap of fabric first. Set the stitch width to about 3 mm (⅛ in) wide and 3 mm (⅛ in) long, then stitch along the raw edges.

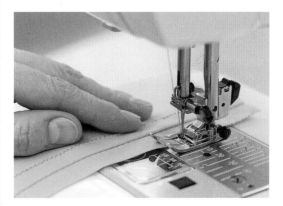

HEMS

Making a Plain Hem

1 Start by pressing under 1 cm (⅜ in) on the raw edge of the fabric. Next, press under the fabric to the depth indicated in the project instructions. Read on if you need to turn a corner, otherwise either stitch close to the inner pressed edge by machine or hand sew in place with a slipstitch or a herringbone stitch, see Hand Stitches.

2 To turn a corner, open out the fabric at the corner and cut diagonally across the seam allowance 6 mm (¼ in) from the corner.

3 Turn the diagonal edge under, then refold the hem, the diagonal folded edges should meet edge to edge. Slipstitch the mitred edges together, see Hand Stitches.

4 Secure the inner pressed edge in place with your chosen method of hemming.

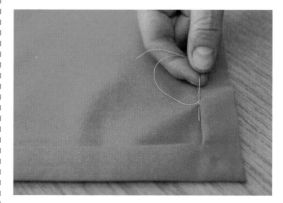

Hemming a Curved Edge

This method will help a curved hem lie flat, on a circular skirt or round tablecloth, for instance. Allow a 1.5cm (⅝ in) hem.

1 Tack (baste) the lower edge by machine 6 mm (¼ in) from the raw edge, starting and finishing at each seam. Fold and pin up a 1.5 cm (⅝ in) hem and tack (baste) by machine close to the folded edge. Gently draw up the first row of tacking to ease the hem so that the eased fabric lies flat.

2 Press the hem, then turn under the raw edge along the eased tacking. Machine stitch close to the inner edge of the hem. Remove both rows of tacking.

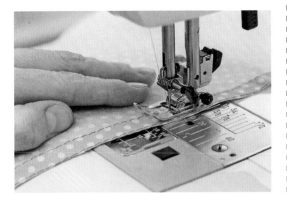

GUSSETS

A gusset is a band of fabric stitched between a front and back piece to create a three-dimensional item.

Turning Gusset Corners

1 With right sides together, stitch the gussets together, starting and finishing the seam at the upper and lower seam allowances. Press the seam open.

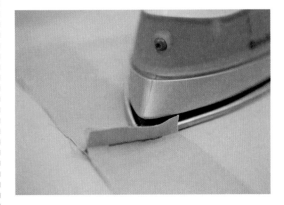

2 Pin the gussets to the main piece of fabric, matching the corners. Stitch, pivoting the seam at the corners.

3 Clip the corners and then press the seam open.

BIAS BINDINGS

Neaten raw edges with a binding, either discreetly to match the fabric or made into a feature with a contrast fabric.

Cutting Bias Strips

The bias is any direction on the fabric that is not the warp and weft. The warp are the woven threads that run parallel with the selvedges and the weft are the woven threads that run at right angles to the selvedge. The true bias is at a 45-degree angle to the warp and weft. It is stretchy, whereas the warp and weft are not, unless the fabric is knitted. Strips of fabric cut on the bias can be used to make bias binding and rouleaux. The bias will cause the seams to stretch so take care when stitching.

Fold the fabric diagonally at a 45-degree angle to the selvedge. Press along the fold then open out flat. Use a fabric marker and ruler to draw lines the width of the binding parallel with the pressed line. To calculate the length needed, add 10 cm (4 in) to the desired length for easing the strip around curves and for tidying the ends. Add a 6 mm (¼ in) seam allowance for joins. Cut out the strips.

Joining Bias Strips

Bias strips are easier to join if the ends are cut diagonally and are therefore cut along the grain line and so not likely to stretch. With right sides together, position one end of two bias strips at right angles, matching the ends. Stitch the strips together taking a 6 mm (¼ in) seam allowance. Press the seam open and clip off the extending corners.

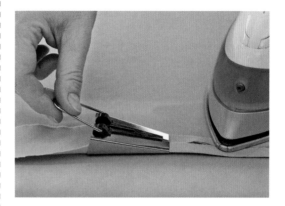

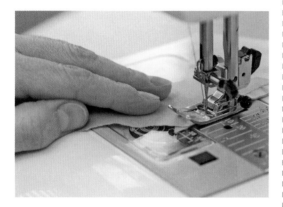

Making Bias Binding

Bias binding makers are gadgets that are available in different widths to make 1.2 cm (½ in), 1.8 cm (¾ in), 2.5 cm (1 in) and 5 cm (2 in) wide bindings. It is useful to have a few of these handy gadgets in different widths. The manufacturer's instructions will indicate the width to cut the binding.

   Resting on an ironing board, push a bias strip of fabric through the wide end of the bias binding maker. The edges will be turned under as the binding emerges out of the narrow end; press in place as you pull the binding through.

Binding a Circumference

Open out one folded edge of the binding, turn under the end to start. With right sides facing, pin the binding to the fabric, matching the raw edges. Pin along the fold line, then cut off the excess binding 1 cm (⅜ in) beyond the start of the binding. Overlap the ends of the strip. Stitch along the fold line.

Binding a Straight Edge

Pin the binding to the fabric, matching the raw edges with the right sides facing and with the ends of the binding extending 1 cm (⅜ in) beyond the ends of the seam. Stitch along the fold line. Turn under both ends of the binding and secure with a pin.

Finishing Binding

Turn the binding to the underside, enclosing the raw edges and matching the pressed edge to the seam. Pin along the seam. Alternatively, turn under the binding so that it is not visible on the right side and pin in place. Slipstitch or stitch along the pressed edge. Slipstitch the ends of the binding in place, see Hand Stitches.

ENVELOPE OPENING

An envelope opening is a flap that closes over the back of a cushion or pillowcase. It is the simplest opening to make on a cushion cover and it allows the cover to be removed easily for laundering.

1 Press under 1 cm (⅜ in) and then 4 cm (1½ in) on one long edge of the flap and the opening edge of the back. Stitch close to the inner pressed edges to hem them.

2 With right sides facing, pin the flap on the front, matching the raw edges. Now, pin the back on top with right sides facing and overlapping the hemmed edges.

3 Stitch the outer edges taking a 1 cm (⅜ in) seam allowance. Clip the corners, then turn right side out.

HANDLES AND TIES

Ribbons and tapes can be used for handles and ties but you can also make your own from strips of fabric.

Press under 1 cm (⅜ in) on the long edges of the fabric strip. For a tie, press under 1 cm (⅜ in) on one end. Press the strip lengthways in half, matching the pressed edges. Stitch close to all pressed edges.

Stitching Ends

Attach the ends of a handle or tie to an item by stitching in all directions in a cross formation within a stitched square. The stitching will secure the handle or tie securely and the cross formation looks attractive too.

1 Press under 1 cm (⅜ in) on the raw ends of the handle or tie. Clip diagonally across the corners.

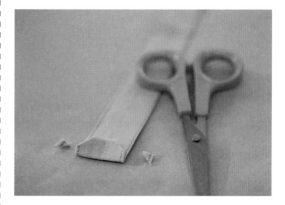

2 Pin the end of the handle or tie to the item. Stitch close to the edges and across the handle or tie, forming a square. Stitch a cross formation diagonally within the square.

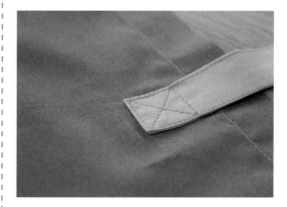

ZIPPERS

A zipper or zip is a neat and inconspicuous closure. Zips are inserted into a seam to fasten a case.

Inserting a Zipper

1 Place the zip centrally under one of the edges it is to be applied to. Mark the position of the outside edge of the top and bottom stops of the zip with a pin.

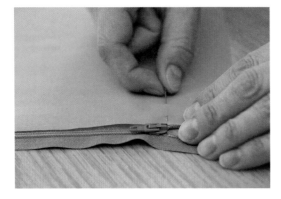

2 With right sides facing, pin the fabric edges together. Stitch each end of the seam, finishing and starting at the pinned marks, taking a 1.5 cm (⅝ in) seam allowance.

3 Next, tack (baste) the seam between the stitching, taking a 1.5 cm (⅝ in) seam allowance.

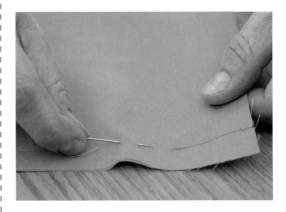

4 Press the seam open. On the wrong side, pin the zip face down centrally along the seam, with one end of the tacked seam level with the inside edge of the end stop at the lower end of the zip. Tack the zip in position.

5 On the right side and starting on one side edge of the zip, use a zipper foot on your sewing machine to stitch it in place 7.5 mm (5⁄16 in) each side of the seam and across the ends of the zip.

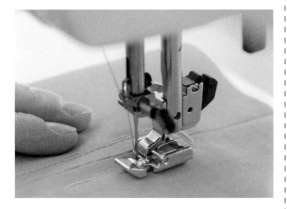

6 Now unpick the tacking and then open the zip. It must be open when stitching your item together, otherwise you won't be able to turn it right side out!

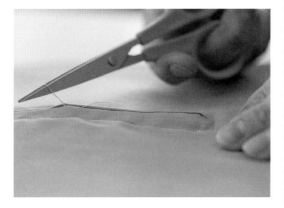

MAKING A ROULEAU

A narrow tube of bias-cut fabric is called a rouleau. Being cut on the bias allows the rouleau to bend easily and to form into pretty petal shapes. When calculating the width to cut the bias strip, double the required width then add two 6 mm (¼ in) seam allowances. Refer to the Cutting Bias Strips technique on page 28.

1 Fold a bias strip of fabric lengthways in half with right sides together. Stitch the long edges, taking a 6 mm (¼ in) seam allowance. Trim the seam allowance if using a 2.5 cm (1 in) wide or narrower bias strip to reduce the bulk of fabric in the rouleau.

2 Turn right side out with a rouleau turner or bodkin. If the rouleau has wrinkled, steam it by holding a steam iron just above the wrinkles. Remove the iron and gently roll the rouleau under the flat palm of your hand.

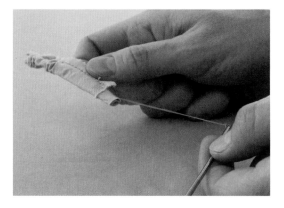

3 The rouleau may have stretched when being turned through. Check the length and trim as required. If necessary, neaten the end of the rouleau by poking the raw end inside with the tip of the closed blades of a pair of embroidery scissors then slipstitching the end closed, see Hand Stitches.

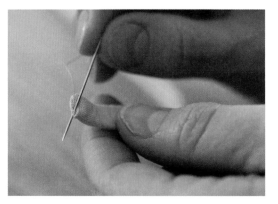

CASINGS

A casing with a drawstring waist on a skirt or a pair of shorts is very forgiving for the wearer and easy to make too. It is a practical design feature if making clothing as a surprise gift as an exact fit isn't necessary. Make the method of opening for the drawstring, for example buttonholes or metal eyelets or by leaving a gap in the seam before stitching the channel.

MAKING A CASING

1 Press under 6 mm (¼ in) on the upper edge and stitch in place.

2 Press under the upper edge for 5 cm (2 in).

3 On the right side, stitch 2 cm (¾ in), then 4 cm (1½ in) below the upper edge to form the channel.

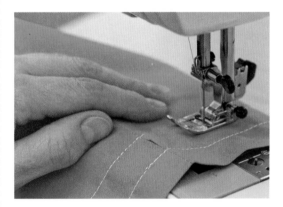

APPLYING RIBBON

To pin ribbon and other trimmings in a straight line, either draw a line with an air-erasable pen to line it up against or push the trimming up against a ruler. Pin the ribbon to the fabric. Stitch close to one edge of the ribbon then close to the other edge of the ribbon. Always stitch both ribbon edges in the same direction, otherwise the ribbon will drag and wrinkle.

Ric-rac braid is applied by stitching along its centre.

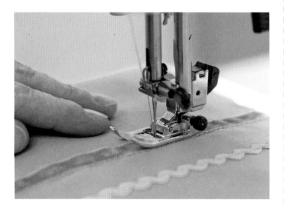

FILLED SHAPES

Always consider how you are going to turn a small shapely item right side out once it is stitched. You will need to leave a gap to turn through. If possible, have the gap on a straight part, as it is easier to slipstitch straight edges closed than curved ones. Alternatively, if the back of the item will not be seen, such as on the Bird Brooch, cut a slit to turn through and oversew the edges closed afterwards.

Making a Filled Shape

1 Stitch the shape, leaving a gap to turn through. If the item is small and curved, keep the stitch length small and stitch slowly for accuracy. Clip the corners and curves.

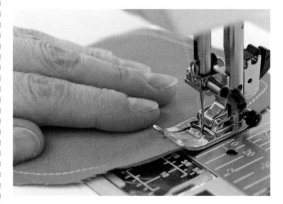

2 Finger press the seams of small shapes open by supporting the seam inside with one hand or finger. Splay the seam open then run a moistened finger of the other hand along the seam. Leave to dry before turning right side out.

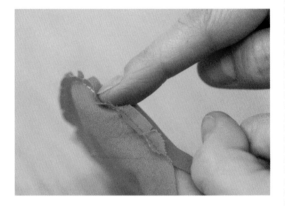

3 Turn the shape to the right side. Turn corners to a point by gently easing the corner into shape with a pin. Don't overwork the corner, as the clipped seam allowance could fray and show on the right side.

4 To stuff the shape with polyester toy filling, tease the stuffing apart before inserting it, avoid pushing in dense lumps of filling or the effect will be bumpy. To push the filling into narrow areas and points, use a rounded tool such as the end of an artist's paintbrush handle – don't use a pointed tool as it could break the stitches.

5 You may wish to fill the shape with other fillings such as potpourri to make a potpourri sachet, or fine sawdust or emery sand powder to make a pin cushion. Roll a piece of paper into a funnel and secure the shape with sticky tape. Insert the narrow end of the funnel into the cavity and pour in the filling. A spoon can be used to tip in the contents, if you prefer.

6 Pin the pressed edges of the gap closed, then slipstitch the edges together, see Hand Stitches. Keep the stitches small if using fine powdery fillings.

TEMPLATES

You will need templates for some of the projects, or to refer to diagrams to make the clothes. Trace the templates onto tracing paper or enlarge on a photocopier where indicated. Remember to transfer any grain lines, fold lines, dots and other useful information onto the template then cut it out.

The clothes diagrams are simple to follow and draw on paper. Making a paper pattern means that you can use it again and again. Start with a rectangle or square of paper drawn to the measurements given, this provides an outline to draw the pattern within. Refer to the diagram to draw the patterns, following the measurements (see right) and shape of the diagram. Draw straight lines against a ruler. Check your measurements again then cut out the pattern.

SIZES

The apron pattern is one-size and the other clothes patterns are sized Small (size 8–10) and Medium (size 10–12). Choose your size from the guidelines given. On the diagrams, Small is given first, then Medium is shown in brackets.

Small

Bust: 84 cm (33 in)
Waist: 62 cm (24½ in)
Hips: 89 cm (34¾ in)

Medium

Bust: 88 cm (34½ in)
Waist: 66 cm (26 in)
Hips: 93 cm (36½ in)

Check the length of the clothes, measure from the nape of the back of your neck for the Cropped T-shirt and T-shirt Dress, measure from your waist for skirts and shorts. It you want to make them longer, simply add extra to the bottom when you cut out, remembering to add the same amount to both the front and the back. If you want the item to be shorter, just trim the surplus off the bottom before you turn up the hem.

The projects

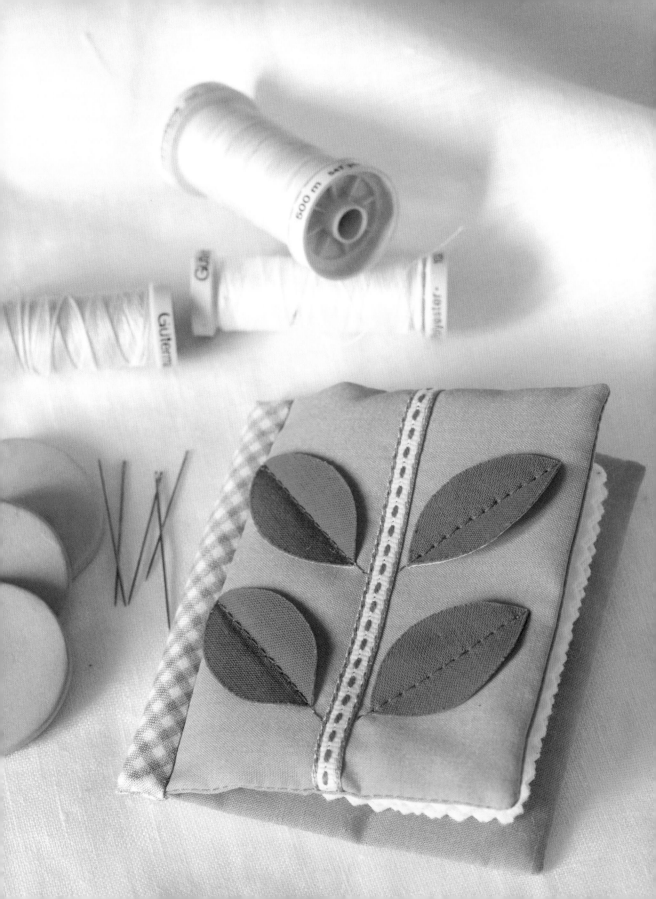

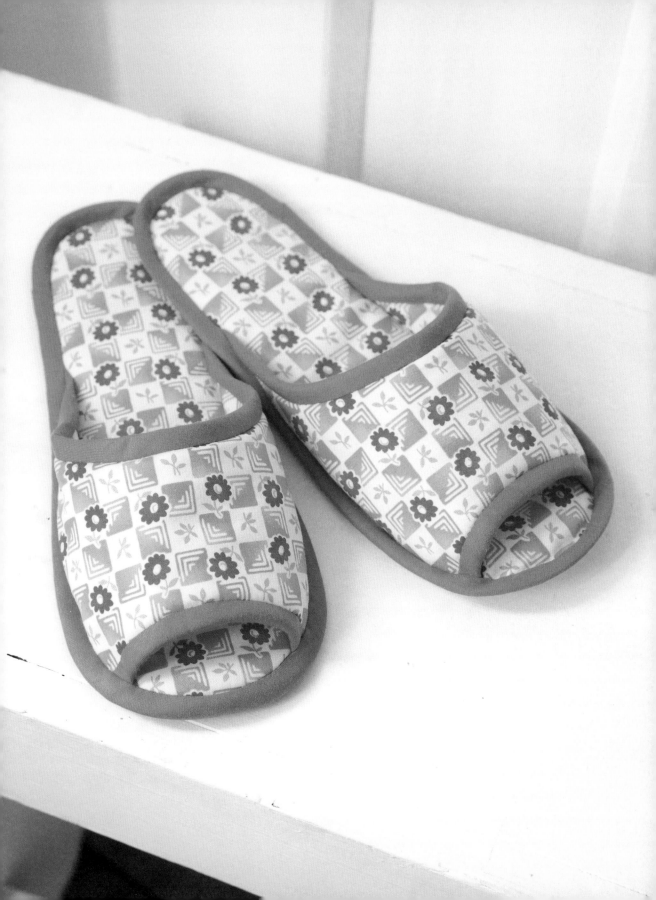

Flared Skirt

This pretty skirt is a great project for a first clothes sewing venture. The four panels gently flare from a drawstring waistline. Ribbon drawstrings are sewn to elastic, which makes the skirt easy and comfortable to wear. This skirt is made in a lively patterned cotton but would also work well in linen or lightweight wool.

You will need

- 1 m 10 cm (1⅓ yd) of 112 cm (44 in)-wide bright blue patterned cotton fabric
- Two 8 mm (⁵⁄₁₆ in) metal eyelets and fixing tool
- 45 cm (½ yd) of 1.5 cm (⅝ in)-wide white elastic
- 1 m 15 cm (1⅓ yd) of 2 cm (¾ in)-wide pale blue chevron ribbon

Cutting out

Refer to the diagram on the following pages.

- For the Small size, make the skirt pattern on a 50 x 18.8 cm (19⅝ x 7⅜ in) rectangle of paper.
- For the Medium size, make the skirt pattern on a 51 x 19.5 cm (20⅛ x 7⅝ in) rectangle of paper.
- From bright blue patterned fabric, cut four skirts to the fold.

1 Tidy the front, back and side edges with a zig-zag stitch (see the Tidying Seams technique on page 25). Pin the skirts together in pairs with right sides together. Stitch one long edge of each pair, taking a 1.5 cm (⅝ in) seam allowance. Press the seams open.

2 On one skirt, follow the manufacturer's instructions to fix an 8 mm (⁵⁄₁₆ in) metal eyelet on each side of the seam with the centre of the eyelet 8 cm (3⅛ in) below the upper edge and 2.2 cm (⅞ in) in from the seam. This will be the front skirt. With right sides facing, pin the skirts together along the long side edges. Stitch the side seams taking a 1.5 cm (⅝ in) seam allowance. Press the seams open.

3 Refer to the Making a Casing technique steps 2–3 on page 35 to make a casing on the upper edge. Cut the ribbon in half. Press under 1 cm (⅜ in) on one end of each ribbon. Overlap the pressed ends over the ends of the elastic by 1 cm (⅜ in). To make the drawstring, stitch close to the pressed edges then 6 mm (¼ in) inside the pressed edges.

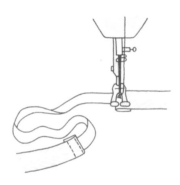

4 Use a bodkin to thread the drawstring through the casing by inserting it through one eyelet and out the other. Adjust the ribbons evenly, cut the ends diagonally. Follow the Making a Hem technique on page 26 to press a 3 cm (1¼ in) deep hem on the lower edge. See the Herringbone Stitch technique on page 23 to sew the hem in place.

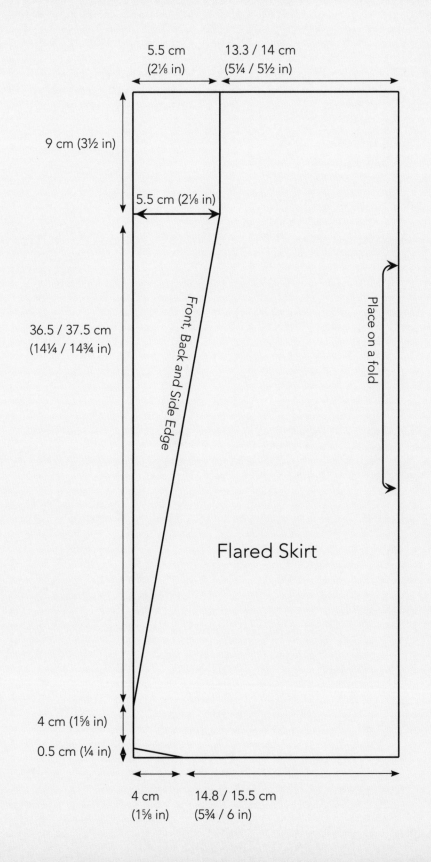

5.5 cm
(2⅛ in)

13.3 / 14 cm
(5¼ / 5½ in)

9 cm (3½ in)

5.5 cm (2⅛ in)

36.5 / 37.5 cm
(14¼ / 14¾ in)

Front, Back and Side Edge

Place on a fold

Flared Skirt

4 cm (1⅝ in)

0.5 cm (¼ in)

4 cm
(1⅝ in)

14.8 / 15.5 cm
(5¾ / 6 in)

Sash Belt

The secret of combining mismatched fabrics is to keep to a similar colour palette. The two fabrics used here give this wrap-around belt a bo-ho style. The belt's long ties wrap around the wide panel to fasten at the front.

You will need

- 20 cm (¼ yd) of 112 cm (44 in)-wide pink patterned cotton fabric
- 30 cm (⅓ yd) of 112 cm (44 in)-wide pink contrasting pattern cotton fabric
- 30 cm (⅓ yd) of 90 cm (36 in)-wide iron-on firm flexible interfacing

Cutting out

- From pink patterned fabric, cut two 105 x 8 cm (41½ x 3⅛ in) strips for the ties.

Refer to the template on the following page.

- From pink contrasting pattern cotton and iron-on firm flexible interfacing fabric, cut one pair of belts, to the fold.

1 Follow the Making a Handle or Tie technique on page 31 to make the ties. Press the interfacing to the wrong side of the belts. Pin and tack (baste) the raw ends of the ties to the centre of the short edges of one belt on the right side.

2 Pin the belts together with right sides facing. Stitch the outer edges taking a 6 mm (¼ in) seam allowance and leaving a 9 cm (3¾ in) gap in the lower edge to turn through, take care not to catch in the extending ends of the ties. Clip the corners and snip the curves then turn the belt right side out. Press the belt. Slipstitch the gap closed, see Hand Stitches.

Enlarge by 178%.

Sash Belt

Place on a fold

Slippers

Don't be daunted by the thought of making slippers; this pair of summer slippers are easy to make. There are patterns for two customised sizes and they are lightweight enough to pop into a travel case to slip into on holidays.

You will need

- 40 cm (½ yd) of 112 cm (44 in)-wide pink patterned cotton fabric
- 50 cm (20 in) square of 70 g (2½ oz) wadding (batting)
- 2 m 10 cm (2⅓ yd) of 1.8 cm (¾ in)-wide pink bias binding
- 30 x 25 cm (12 x 10 in) rectangle of calico (muslin)
- 30 x 25 cm (12 x 10 in) rectangle of iron-on ultra-heavy interfacing
- 30 x 25 cm (12 x 10 in) rectangle of pelmet-weight (craft) interfacing

Cutting out

Refer to the templates on the following page. Size Small (UK 3–4, Eur 37–38) is shown with a solid line, size Medium (UK 5–6, Eur 38–39) is shown with a broken line.

- From pink patterned fabric, cut two pairs of uppers and one pair of soles.
- From wadding (batting), cut one pair of uppers and one pair of soles.
- From calico, cut one pairs of soles.
- From iron-on ultra-heavy interfacing and pelmet interfacing, cut one pair of insoles.

1 Pin and tack (baste) each wadding upper between a pair of fabric uppers with the right sides facing out.

2 Open out one folded edge of bias binding and pin to the toe and inner edges with right sides facing and matching the raw edges. Cut the toe binding level with the side edges and cut across the inner edge bindings level with tips of the inner edges. Stitch along the foldlines. Follow the Finishing Binding technique on page 30 to slipstitch the binding along the seam on the underside of the uppers. Trim the ends of the bindings level with the side edges.

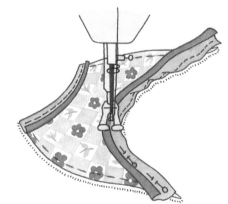

3 Press each iron-on ultra-heavy interfacing insole to a pelmet interfacing insole to fuse the layers together. Tack the wadding soles to the wrong side of the patterned fabric soles. Place the insoles centrally on the wrong side of the calico soles, place the wadded fabric soles right side up on top. Pin and tack the layers together taking a 6 mm (¼ in) seam allowance, to enclose the insoles.

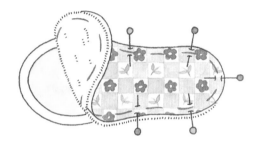

4 With right sides face up, pin and tack the side edges of the uppers to the soles between the dots. Follow the Binding a Circumference technique on page 29 to bind the raw edges.

Adjusting the Pattern

Two sizes are given for the slipper templates but they can be adjusted for a customised fit. Cut an insole from scrap paper and mark the 'lengthen and shorten' line. If it is too short for your foot, cut along the 'lengthen and shorten' line and stick a strip of paper in the gap to lengthen the pattern. If the insole is too long for your foot, fold under the excess length along the 'lengthen and shorten' line. Adjust the sole templates by the same amount.

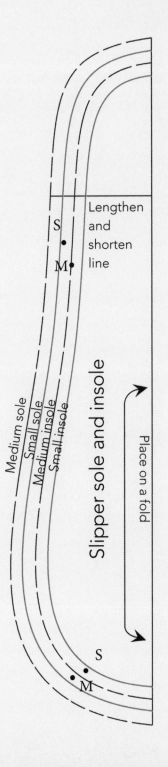

Lengthen and shorten line

S

M

Medium sole

Small sole

Medium insole

Small insole

Slipper sole and insole

Place on a fold

S

M

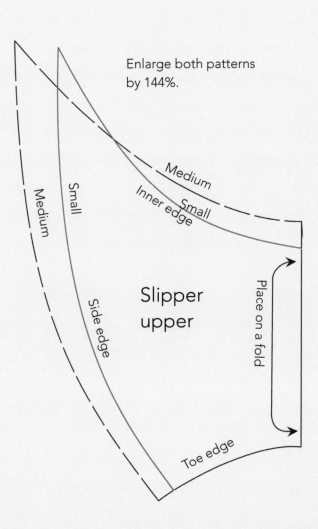

Enlarge both patterns by 144%.

Medium

Inner edge

Small

Medium

Small

Side edge

Slipper upper

Place on a fold

Toe edge

Sleep Mask

Pamper yourself and relax with an unashamedly girly sleep mask. They are simple to create and great to give as gifts. The mask is softly padded with wadding and trimmed with a ribbon bow.

You will need

- 25 cm (10 in) square of purple patterned cotton fabric
- 25 x 15 cm (10 x 6 in) rectangle of 125 g (4 oz) wadding (batting)
- 40 cm (½ yd) of 4 cm (1½in)-wide stretch lace
- 60 cm (⅔ yd) of 1.8 cm (1⅟₁₆ in)-wide lilac bias binding
- 40 cm (½ yd) of 2.5 cm (1 in)-wide lilac chevron ribbon

Cutting out

Refer to the template on the following pages.

- From purple patterned fabric cut one pair of sleep masks to the fold.
- From wadding, cut one sleep mask to the fold.

1 Place the wadding between the fabric masks with the right sides facing outwards. Pin the layers together, smoothing the fabrics out from the centre. Tack (baste) the outer edges by machine or by hand.

2 Cut a 34 cm (13½ in) length of stretch lace. Pin and stitch each end of the lace to the wrong side of the mask at the dots.

3 Refer to the Binding a Circumference and Finishing Binding techniques on pages 29 and 30 to bind the outer edge of the sleep mask. Tie the ribbon in a bow and trim the tails diagonally. Sew the bow to the upper edge of the sleep mask at the left-hand edge.

Sleep Mask

Actual size

Place on a fold

Phone Case

Slip your cell phone into this smart padded case. A layer of wadding gives protection and a popper fastening tab keeps the phone in place but gives easy access.

You will need

- 25 x 20 cm (10 x 8 in) rectangle of grey/peach patterned cotton fabric
- 25 cm (10 in) square of grey plain cotton fabric
- 10 cm (4 in) square of iron-on medium-weight interfacing
- 25 x 20 cm (10 x 8 in) rectangle of 70 g (2½ oz) wadding (batting)
- One popper fastener and fixing tool

Cutting out

- From grey/peach patterned fabric cut two pieces 16.5 x 11 cm (6½ x 4⅜ in) for the front and back cases. Cut the same from wadding.
- From plain grey fabric cut two pieces 8 x 4.5 cm (3¼ x 1¾ in) for the tabs. Cut two pieces 16.5 x 11 cm (6½ x 4⅜ in) for the linings.
- From iron-on medium-weight interfacing cut one square 3 cm (1¼ in) for the popper reinforcement. Cut one piece 8 x 4.5 cm (3¼ x 1¾ in) for the tab.

1 Press the popper reinforcement centrally to the wrong side of the front case and 2 cm (¾ in) below the short upper edge.

2 Press the interfacing to the wrong side of one tab. Pin the tabs together with right sides facing. Taking a 6 mm (¼ in) seam allowance, stitch the tabs together, leaving one short end open. Clip the corners and turn right side out. Press the tab.

3 Follow the manufacturer's instructions to fix the male section of the popper at the centre of the popper reinforcement and the female section of the popper to the tab matching the centre of the popper 2 cm (¾ in) in from the finished end of the tab.

4 Tack (baste) the grey / peach front and back case pieces right side up on the wadding pieces. With right sides together, pin and tack the raw end of the tab to the short upper edge of the back case.

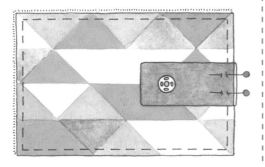

5 Pin each case to a lining with right sides together at the short upper edges only, taking a 1 cm (⅜ in) seam allowance. Stitch in place. Carefully trim away the wadding in the seam allowance to reduce the bulk. Open out and press the seams toward the linings.

6 With right sides together, pin the opened out cases and linings, right sides together and matching the seams. Stitch the outer edges, taking a 1 cm (⅜ in) seam allowance, leaving a 9 cm (3¾ in) gap in one long edge of the lining to turn through.

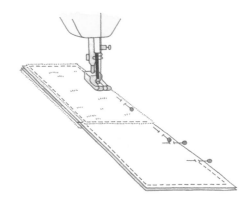

7 Carefully trim away the wadding in the seam allowance. Clip all four corners and turn right side out. Slipstitch the gap closed (see Hand Stitches). Push the lining into the case and press the upper edge.

Laptop Case

This elegant laptop case will hold a 25 cm (10 in) computer comfortably. A magnetic closure gives a professional finish to the case and provides a secure fastening that is quick and easy to open.

You will need

- 60 x 35 cm (23½ x 14 in) rectangle of light green plain linen fabric
- 30 cm (12 in) square of grey patterned cotton fabric
- 50 cm (½ yd) of 90 cm (36 in)-wide iron-on firm flexible interfacing
- 60 x 35 cm (23½ x 14 in) rectangle of iron-on medium loft fleece
- 60 x 35 cm (23½ x 14 in) rectangle of white plain cotton fabric
- One set of magnetic snap closures

Cutting out

- From light green plain fabric, cut two pieces 34 x 29 cm (13⅜ x 11½ in) for the front and back case. Cut the same from iron-on firm flexible interfacing, iron-on medium loft fleece and white plain fabric.

Refer to the template on the following page.

- From grey patterned fabric cut one pair of flaps to the fold. Cut the same from iron-on firm flexible interfacing.

1 Press the iron-on firm flexible interfacing to the wrong side of the light green front and back case and the flaps. Next, press iron-on fleece to the interfaced side of the cases.

2 Place one washer of the magnetic snap closure on the centre on the right side of the light green front with the centre of the washer 8 cm (3¼ in) below the long upper edge. Mark the position of the slots with an air-erasable pen. Centre one washer at the cross position on the right side of one flap, mark the slots as before. Carefully cut slits through the fleece, interfacing and fabric. Insert the prongs of the closure through the slits to the wrong side placing the female section on the front and male section on the flap. Insert the prongs through the washers then splay the prongs open with a pair of pliers. Flatten the prongs with the pliers.

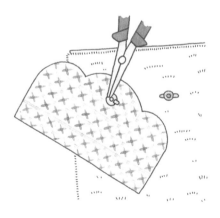

3 Pin the flaps together with right sides facing. Stitch the flaps taking a 6 mm (¼ in) seam allowance and leaving the back edge open. Clip the seam allowance to the corners of the scallops and clip the curves. Turn the flap right side out and press flat. Pin the raw edges together. With right sides facing, pin and tack (baste) the flap centrally to the long upper edge of the light green back, matching the raw edges.

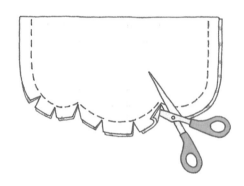

4 With right sides facing, pin the light green cases together. Stitch the case, taking a 1 cm (⅜ in) seam allowance and leaving the long upper edge open. Clip the corners and press the seams open.

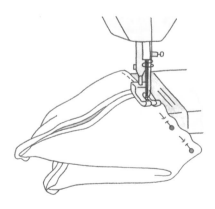

5 Repeat to make the lining from the white rectangles, leaving an 18 cm (7 in) gap in one edge to turn through. Turn the case right side out. Slip the case into the lining, matching the seams and raw edges. Remove the bed of the sewing machine. Slip the case over the arm of the machine and stitch the raw edges taking a 1 cm (⅜ in) seam allowance. Turn the lining to the right side. Slipstitch the gap in the lining closed (see Hand Stitches). Push the lining into the case and press the opening edge. Topstitch the case 7.5 mm (⁹⁄₁₆ in) inside the opening edges.

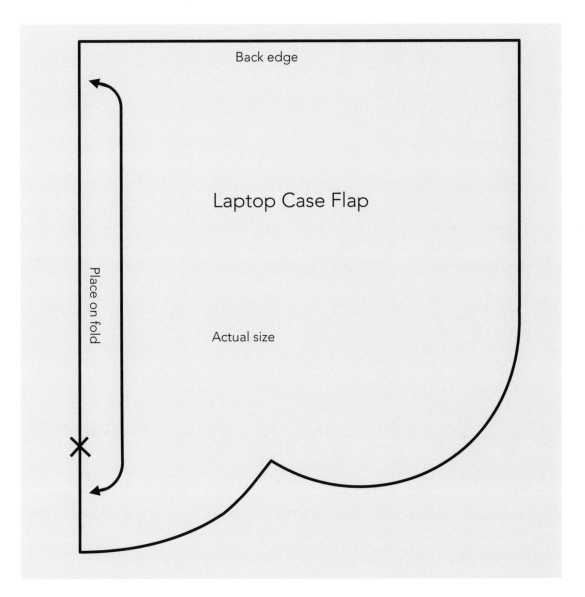

Back edge

Place on fold

Laptop Case Flap

Actual size

E-book Case

Choose a bright, cheery fabric to make this practical case for an e-book. The case is softly padded and fastens with a ribbon and D-rings. It's an easy project that can be used for other purposes too, such as storing recipe cards or stationery. Simply change the size of the case to suit your needs.

You will need
- 35 x 25 cm (14 x 10 in) rectangle of pink / grey patterned cotton fabric
- 35 x 25 cm (14 x 10 in) rectangle of grey plain cotton fabric
- 35 x 25 cm (14 x 10 in) rectangle of iron-on medium-loft fleece
- 45 cm (½ yd) of 2.5 cm (1 in)-wide pink grosgrain ribbon
- Two 2.5 cm (1 in) D-rings

Cutting out
- From patterned fabric, cut one 30 x 23 cm (12 x 9 in) rectangle for the case.
- Cut the same from plain fabric and iron-on medium-loft fleece.

1 Press iron-on fleece to the wrong side of the patterned case. Slip two D-rings onto a 6 cm (2⅜ in) length of ribbon and pin the ends together. Pin the ribbon to the right side of the patterned case at the centre of one short edge with the raw edges level. Pin one end of the remaining ribbon on top. Tack (baste) the raw ends in place.

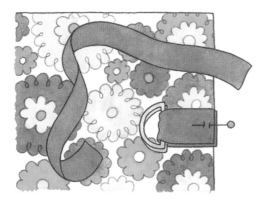

2 With right sides facing, fold the patterned case in half parallel with the short edges. Stitch the top and bottom edges taking a 1 cm (⅜ in) seam allowance. Clip the corners and press the seams open.

3 Repeat to make the lining from the grey rectangle, leaving an 11 cm (4¼ in) gap in one edge to turn through. Turn the case right side out. Slip the case into the lining matching the seams and raw edges. Remove the bed of the sewing machine. Slip the case over the arm of the machine and stitch the raw edges taking a 1cm (⅜ in) seam allowance. Turn the lining to the right side. Slipstitch the gap closed (see Hand Stitches).

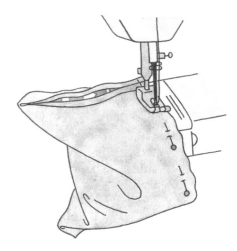

4 Push the lining into the case and press the opening edge. Topstitch the case 7.5 mm (⁹⁄₁₆ in) inside the opening edges. Cut the end of the ribbon diagonally.

Travel Tissue Case

You'll find your pack of tissues easily if you keep them protected in a brightly patterned case attached with a swivel bolt snap to the zipper pull of an inner pocket in your handbag. This case is a quick make that uses a small amount of fabric and bias binding.

You will need
- 20 cm (8 in) square of pink patterned cotton fabric
- 35 cm (14 in) of 2.5 cm (1 in)-wide co-ordinating bias binding
- One swivel bolt snap

Cutting out
- From pink patterned fabric, cut one 15 cm (6 in) square for the case.

1 Press 2.5 cm (1 in)-wide bias binding lengthwise in half with wrong sides facing. Cut two 15 cm (6 in) lengths of the binding. Slip two opposite edges of the case into the bindings, pin and tack in place. Stitch close to the inner edges of the binding on the right side of the case.

2 Stitch close to both long edges of the remaining binding to make the swivel bolt snap holder. Slip the swivel bolt snap onto the holder and pin the ends together. Pin and tack (baste) the ends of the holder to the right side of the case beside one bound edge.

3 Mark the centre of the raw edges of the case with a pin. With right sides facing, bring the bound edges to meet at the pins. Pin the raw edges together. Stitch the raw edges, taking a 6 mm (¼ in) seam allowance, stitching back and forwards a few times where the bindings meet to reinforce the seams. Zig-zag stitch the raw edges of the seams together to tidy them. Turn the case right side out ready to slip a travel pack of tissues inside.

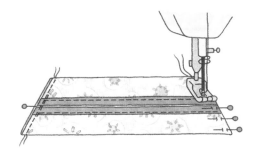

Cloud Lavender Sachet

Too sweet to hide in a drawer, hang this fragrant cloud-shaped sachet on a clothes hanger to freshen your clothes. The cloud has an embroidered shy smile and heart-shaped button eyes.

You will need

- 20 x 15 cm (8 x 6 in) rectangle of light blue plain cotton fabric
- Pink stranded embroidery cotton
- Size 8 crewel embroidery needle
- Two 6 mm (¼ in) purple heart-shaped buttons
- 20 cm (¼ yd) of 6 mm (¼in)-wide pink Funny Road ribbon
- One 8 mm (⁵⁄₁₆ in) pale blue star button
- 6 g (¼ oz) dried lavender flowerheads
- Piece of scrap paper and sticky tape

Cutting out

Refer to the template on the following page.

- From light blue plain fabric, cut one pair of clouds.

1 Draw the smile and dots on the right side of one cloud with an air-erasable pen. Thread a crewel embroidery needle with three strands of pink stranded embroidery cotton. Knot the ends and bring the thread to the right side at the centre of the smile, make a stitch to one end of the smile. Bring the needle to the right side at the centre and make another stitch to the other end of the smile. Fasten the thread on the underside of the cloud. Sew a heart button at each dot for eyes.

2 Pin the clouds together with right sides facing. Follow the Making a Filled Shape technique on page 36 to stitch the clouds together taking a 6 mm (¼ in) seam allowance and filling the sachet with dried lavender seeds. Overlap the ends of the ribbon by 2 cm (¾ in) and sew to the top of the cloud. Sew a star-shaped button on top. Cut the ribbon ends diagonally.

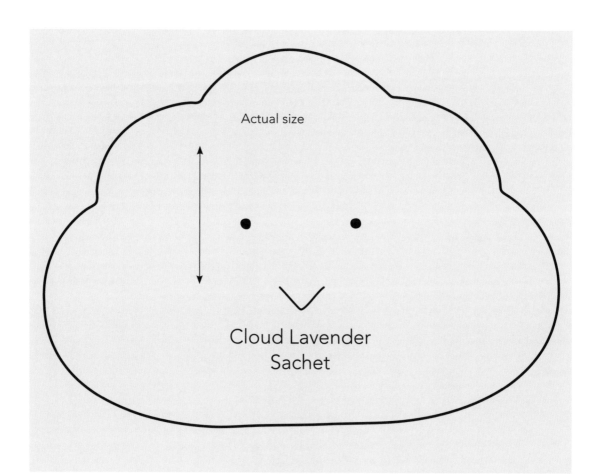

Actual size

Cloud Lavender
Sachet

Foxy Key Fob

You'll never loose keys if you add them to this bold felt foxy key fob. Felt crafts are very popular and it's easy to see why. Felt is great to work with, cheap to buy and comes in a huge range of colours. Layers of felt are fused with bonding web to make the fob robust and practical.

You will need

- 20 x 10 cm (8 x 4 in) rectangle of brown felt
- 5 cm (2 in) square white felt
- 15 x 10 cm (6 x 4 in) rectangle of fusible bonding web
- One 6 mm (¼ in) metal eyelet and fixing tool
- Two 3 mm (⅛ in) black round buttons
- One 6 mm (¼ in) black heart button
- One key ring

Cutting out

Refer to the template on the following page.

- From brown felt, cut two 10 cm (4 in) squares for the key fob.
- From bonding web, cut one 10 cm (4 in) square for the key fob.

1 Press one square of brown felt right side up on the square of fusible bonding web. Peel off the backing paper. Position the other felt square on top and press to fuse the layers together.

2 Refer to the template to cut the fox from tracing paper, mark the cheeks, broken lines and dots for the eyes and cross. Draw around the template on the brown felt square with a sharp HB pencil. Trace the cheek templates onto the paper backing of a piece of fusible bonding web. Roughly cut out the fusible web cheeks leaving a margin all around. Press the cheeks on to white felt then cut them out. Peel off the paper backing. Arrange the cheeks in position on the fox. Press the pieces to fuse the layers together.

3 Stitch close to the inner edges of the cheeks. Refer to the template to stitch along the broken lines and close to the pencil line between the ears. Stitch close to the inside edge of the fox outline. Carefully cut out the fox along the drawn outline.

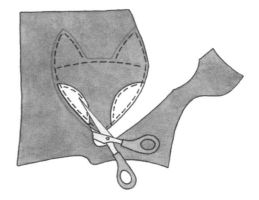

4 Fix a metal eyelet at the cross. Sew black round buttons at the dots and a heart button at the tip for a nose. Fix a key ring through the eyelet.

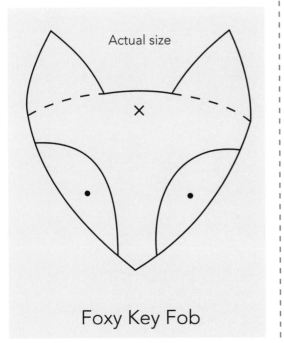

Actual size

×

Foxy Key Fob

Needle Case

Keep your sewing needles safe in a pretty needle case. The front cover has a simple bold decoration of fabric leaves and ribbon. The 'hinge' of the case is bound with gingham bias binding. Remember that you can make your own bias binding, see the technique on page 29.

You will need

- 25 cm (10 in) square of turquoise plain cotton fabric
- 15 cm (⅙ yd) of 6 mm (¼ in) wide white Funny Road ribbon
- 10 cm (4 in) square of teal plain cotton fabric
- 10 cm (4 in) square of iron-on firm interfacing
- 25 x 15 cm (10 x 6 in) rectangle of 70 g (2½ oz) wadding (batting)
- 20 cm (8 in) square of white felt
- 15 cm (⅙ yd) of 2.5 cm (1 in)-wide lilac gingham bias binding

Cutting out

- From turquoise plain cotton fabric cut four pieces 12 x 10 cm (4¾ x 4in) for the front and back covers.

Refer to the template on the following pages.

- Press interfacing to the wrong side of teal plain fabric. From interfaced fabric, cut four leaves.
- From wadding, cut two 12 x 10 cm (4¾ x 4 in) rectangles for the front and back covers.
- From white felt, cut four rectangles 8.5 x 8 cm (3½ x 3¼ in) for the pages using pinking shears.

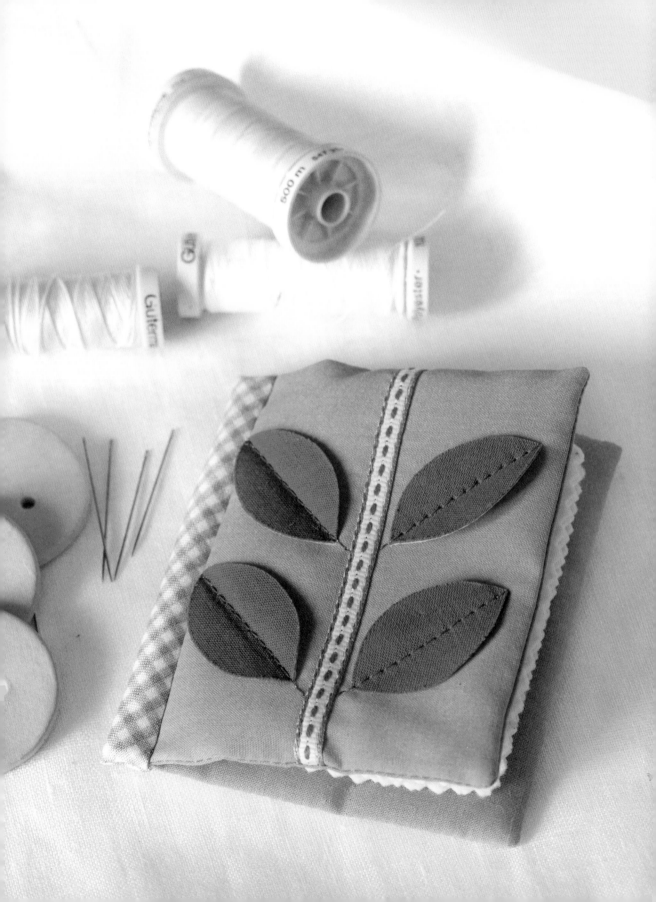

1 Apply 6 mm (¼ in) wide white Funny Road ribbon along the centre on the right side of one turquoise cover, parallel with the long side edges, following the Applying Ribbon technique on page 36.

2 Press the leaves in half along the broken lines with right sides facing then open out flat again. Arrange two leaves on each side of the ribbon 'stem' keeping the leaves within the 1 cm (⅜ in) seam allowance. Pin and tack (baste) the leaves in place. Stitch along the foldlines, continuing the stitches to reach the ribbon. Pull the thread ends to the wrong side of the cover and fasten. This will be the front cover.

3 Pin and tack the wadding to the wrong side of the front cover and one other cover which will be the back cover. With right sides facing, pin the remaining covers to the front and back. Stitch the covers together leaving the long left-hand edge of the front case and the long right-hand edge of the back cover open, taking a 1 cm (⅜ in) seam allowance. Carefully trim away the wadding in the seam allowance. Clip the corners.

4 Turn the front and back covers right side out. Tack the raw edges together. Pile the pages on top of the back cover, matching one long edge of the pages centrally on the raw edge. Place the front, right side up on top matching the raw edges. Pin and tack the left-hand edges together. Follow the Binding a Straight Edge and Finishing Binding techniques on page 30 to bind the left-hand edge.

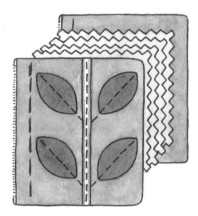

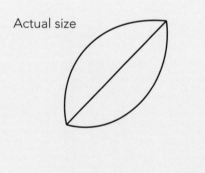

Actual size

Needle Case Leaf

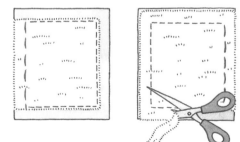

Shorts

Shorts are here to stay and this smart pair looks good with all sorts of tops. The drawstring waist is flattering and is kept in place with matching ties that fasten at the front.

You will need
- 1 m 20 cm (1½ yd) of 112 cm (44 in)-wide grey patterned cotton fabric
- 45 cm (½ yd) of 1.5 cm (⅝ in)-wide white elastic

Cutting out
Refer to the diagram on the following pages.
- For the Small size, make the pattern for the front shorts on a 53 x 33 cm (21 x 13 in) rectangle of paper and a pattern for the back shorts on a 55.5 x 39.5 cm (22 x 15⅝ in) rectangle of paper.
- For the Medium size, make the pattern for the front shorts on a 54 x 34 cm (21⅜ x 13⅜ in) rectangle of paper and a pattern for the back shorts on a 56.5 x 40.5 cm (22⅜ x 16 in) rectangle of paper.
- From grey patterned cotton fabric, cut one pair of front shorts and one pair of back shorts. Cut two strips for the ties 58 x 5 cm (23 x 2 in).

1 Tidy the raw edges of the centre front, centre back, side and inner leg edges with a zig-zag stitch (see the Neatening Seams technique).

2 On the front shorts, follow the Making a Buttonhole technique to make a 1.5 cm (⅝ in)-long vertical buttonhole with the top of the buttonhole 7.2 cm (2⅞ in) below the upper edge and 3 cm (1¼ in) in from the centre front edge.

3 Pin the front shorts and back shorts together in pairs with right sides facing. Stitch the centre front and back seams taking a 1.5 cm (⅝ in) seam allowance. Press the seams open, the curved edges will not lie completely flat so run the toe of the iron along the line of the seam itself.

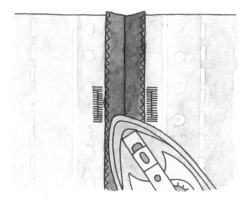

4 With right sides facing, pin the front shorts to the back shorts along the side edges. Stitch the side seams taking a 1.5 cm (⅝ in) seam allowance. Pin and stitch the inner leg edges together with right sides facing, matching the centre front and back seams and taking a 1.5 cm (⅝ in) seam allowance. Press the side and inner leg seams open.

5 Refer to the Making a Casing technique on page 35 to make a casing on the upper edge. Follow the Making a Handle or Tie technique on page 31 to make the ties. Press under 1 cm (⅜ in) on the raw end of each tie. Overlap the pressed ends over the ends of the elastic by 1 cm (⅜ in).

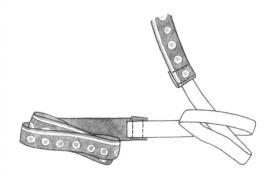

6 To make the drawstring, stitch close to the pressed ends then 6 mm (¼ in) inside the pressed ends. Use a bodkin to thread the drawstring through the casing by inserting it through one buttonhole and out the other. Follow the Making a Hem technique on page 26 to press a 3 cm (1¼ in) deep hem on the lower edges. See the Herringbone Stitch technique on page 23 to sew the hem in place.

Girl's Guide to Sewing

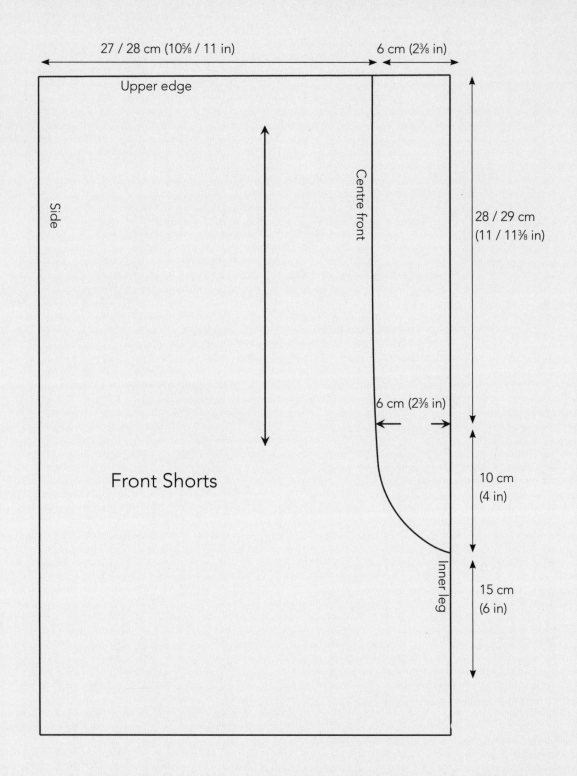

27 / 28 cm (10⅝ / 11 in)

6 cm (2⅜ in)

Upper edge

Side

Centre front

28 / 29 cm
(11 / 11⅜ in)

6 cm (2⅜ in)

Front Shorts

10 cm
(4 in)

Inner leg

15 cm
(6 in)

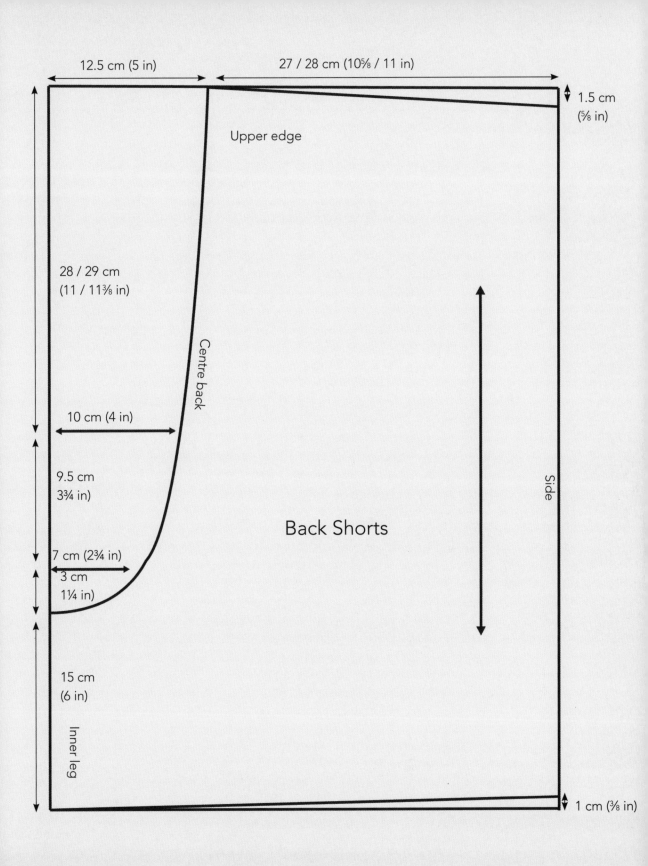

12.5 cm (5 in)

27 / 28 cm (10⅝ / 11 in)

1.5 cm (⅝ in)

Upper edge

28 / 29 cm (11 / 11⅜ in)

Centre back

10 cm (4 in)

9.5 cm 3¾ in)

Back Shorts

Side

7 cm (2¾ in)

3 cm 1¼ in)

15 cm (6 in)

Inner leg

1 cm (⅜ in)

Hedgehog Pin Cushion

This adorable little hedgehog is not only cute but practical too, keeping your sewing pins and needles safe. Glass-headed pins form a crowning glory of colourful spines. A sawdust or emery sand powder filling prevents pins and needles from rusting and adds some weight so that the pin cushion will sit steadily on your work surface.

You will need
- 20 x 15 cm (8 x 6 in) rectangle of pale turquoise plain cotton fabric
- 20 x 15 cm (8 x 6 in) rectangle of turquoise patterned cotton fabric
- 5 cm (2 in) square of pale grey felt
- 25 g (1 oz) sawdust or emery sand powder
- One 6 mm (¼ in) black bead
- Piece of scrap paper and sticky tape
- Two black glass-headed pins
- Turquoise glass-headed pins

Cutting out
Refer to the templates on the following page.
- From pale turquoise plain fabric: cut one head to the fold. Cut one base to the fold.
- From pale grey felt, cut one pair of ears.
- From turquoise patterned fabric, cut one pair of bodies.

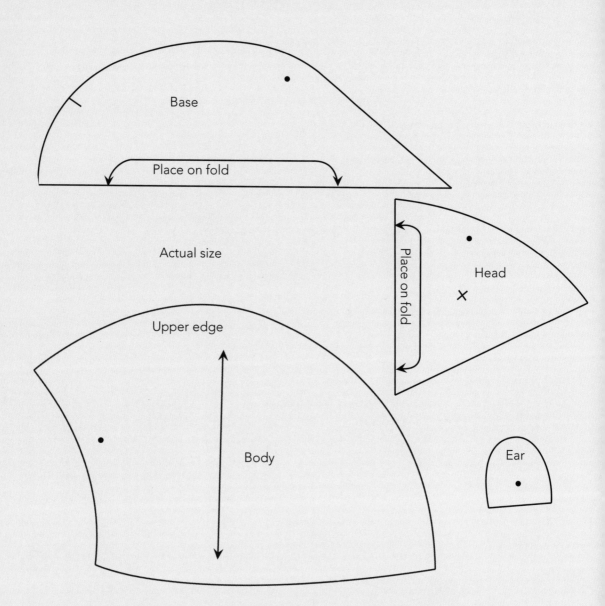

Base

Place on fold

Actual size

Place on fold

Head

Upper edge

Body

Ear

Hedghog Pin Cushion

1 With right sides facing up, pin and tack (baste) the ears to the head matching the dots. With right sides facing, pin and stitch the bodies together along the upper edge taking a 6 mm (¼ in) seam allowance. Clip the curves then press the seam open.

2 With right sides facing, pin the head to the body matching the dots. Taking a 6 mm (¼ in) seam allowance, stitch the body to the head. Clip the curves. Press the seam toward the head.

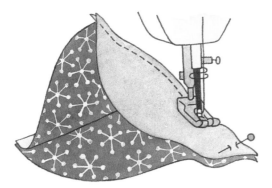

3 Pin the body and head to the base matching the dots to the head seam and notches. Stitch the outer edge. taking a 6 mm (¼ in) seam allowance leaving a gap to turn through. Clip the corner and clip the curves.

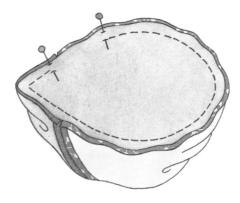

4 Follow steps 3–6 of the Making a Filled Shape technique on page 36 to fill the hedgehog with sawdust or emery sand powder and slipstitch the gap closed. Sew a 6 mm (¼ in) bead to the tip of the head for the nose. Insert two black glass-headed pins into the head at the crosses as eyes, angling the pins in toward the body. Insert turquoise glass-headed pins into the body to represent the hedgehog's spines.

Table Coaster

Appliqué perse is a very old needlecraft technique in which motifs are cut from printed motif fabric and embroidered onto a plain fabric. Bring the technique up-to-date with this vibrant drinks coaster. A stylized apple has been used here for the motif. Kitchen towels are good sources of cheap, brightly printed and quirky motifs.

You will need

- 9 cm (3½ in) square of apple-patterned cotton fabric with the motif centred
- 9 cm (3½ in) square of fusible bonding web
- 12 cm (4¾ in) square of insulated wadding (batting)
- 30 x 15 cm (12 x 6 in) rectangle of green plain linen fabric
- Co-ordinating coloured stranded embroidery cotton
- Size 8 crewel embroidery needle

Cutting out

- From green plain fabric, cut two 12 cm (4¾ in) squares for the coaster

Tip... Insulated wadding is heat resistant but not heatproof. Curtain interlining can be used instead but it offers less heat resistance.

1 Press the square of patterned fabric right side up on the square of bonding web. Turn the piece over and press again to fuse the layers together. Cut out the apple motif neatly. Peel off the backing paper. Position the motif on the centre of the right side of one coaster. Press the motif to the coaster.

2 Thread a size 8 crewel needle with two strands of embroidery thread, knot the end. Blanket stitch the outer edge of the apple. To blanket stitch, bring the needle out on the edge of the motif then insert it 3 mm (⅛ in) to the right-hand side and 3 mm (⅛ in) in from the edge. Bring the needle out on the edge of the motif, 3 mm (⅛ in) along from where it first emerged, keeping the thread under the needle. Pull the needle and thread through the fabric and continue all around the edge of the apple (see page 92 for blanket stitch diagram). Blanket stitch along the stalk too.

3 Tack the insulated wadding to the wrong side of the appliquéd coaster. Pin the fabric coasters together with right sides facing. Stitch the raw edges taking a 1 cm (⅜ in) seam allowance, leaving a 6 cm (2½ in) gap in one edge to turn through. Carefully trim away the wadding in the seam allowance close to the seam and gap to reduce the bulk in the seam allowance. Clip the corners. Turn the coaster right side out and press the edges. Slipstitch the gap closed (see Hand Stitches).

Ribbon Flags Cushion

The combination of two vibrant fabrics on this funky cushion will brighten any room. The row of colourful flags are easy to make from folded lengths of ribbons and an envelope back allows you to remove the cushion cover easily for laundering.

You will need

- 50 x 30 cm (20 x 12 in) rectangle of green spotted cotton fabric
- 50 cm (½ yd) of 112 cm (44 in) wide green/turquoise patterned cotton fabric
- 60 cm (⅔ yd) of turquoise 2.5 cm (1 in)-wide stitched edge ribbon
- 50 cm (½ yd) of turquoise 2.2 cm (¾ in)-wide patterned ribbon
- 40 cm (16 in) square cushion pad

Cutting out

- From green spotted fabric, cut one piece 42 x 28.5 cm (16¾ x 11¼ in) for the front.
- From green/turquoise patterned fabric, cut one piece 42 x 15.5 cm (16¾ x 6¼ in) for the band. Cut one square 42 cm (16¾ in) for the back, and one piece 42 x 19 cm (16¾ x 7½ in) for the flap.

1 From turquoise 2.5 cm (1 in)-wide stitched-edge ribbon, cut seven lengths each 8 cm (3⅛ in). Fold the ribbons in half with wrong sides facing and pin the ends together. Pin and tack (baste) the ribbons in a row to one long edge on the right side of the cushion front, placing the ribbons equidistant and 6 cm (2⅜ in) in from the short side edges.

2 With right sides facing, pin and stitch one long edge of the band to the long upper edge of the front taking a 1 cm (⅜ in) seam allowance and catching the raw edges of the ribbon in the seam. Press the seam toward the band.

3 Follow the Applying Ribbons technique on page 36 to stitch turquoise 2.2 cm (¾ in) wide patterned ribbon to the band along the seam.

4 Follow the Envelope Opening technique on page 30 to make the cushion.

Pencil Case

Use this smart pencil case to keep pens and pencils together and quick to find. The case is softly padded and has a ribbon pull to make the zip fastening easy to open and close. Of course the case can also be used for other purposes; it would be a neat make-up or sewing case.

You will need

- 35 x 25 cm (14 x 10 in) rectangle of fawn-patterned cotton fabric
- 40 x 25 cm (16 x 10 in) rectangle of light green plain cotton fabric
- 18 cm (7in) zipper
- 40 x 25 cm (16 x 10 in) rectangle of iron-on medium loft fleece
- 10 cm (4 in) of 1 cm (⅜ in)-wide striped grosgrain ribbon

Cutting out

- From fawn-patterned fabric and iron-on medium loft fleece, cut one 23 x 13 cm (9¼ x 5¼ in) rectangle for the front. Cut one 23 x 17 cm (9¼ x 6¾ in) rectangle for the back.
- From light green plain fabric, cut two 23 x 7 cm (9½ x 2¾ in) rectangles for the band and band lining. Cut one 23 x 13 cm (9¼ x 5¼ in) rectangle for the front lining. Cut one 23 x 17 cm (9¼ x 6¾ in) rectangle for the back lining.

1 Press the iron-on medium loft fleece pieces to the wrong side of the front, back and band.

2 Follow the Inserting a zip (zipper) technique on page 32 to insert the zip centrally between one long edge of the band and front.

3 With right sides facing, pin and stitch the front and band to the back along the outer edges taking a 1.5 cm (⅝ in) seam allowance. Clip the corners. Press the seams open.

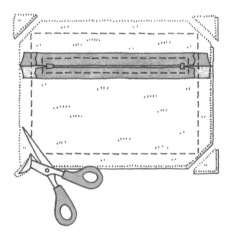

4 With right sides facing, take a 1.5 cm (⅝ in) seam allowance to stitch the band lining to the front lining along one long edge leaving an 18 cm (7 in) gap in the centre. Press the seam open. Pin and stitch the front lining and band lining to the back lining along the outer edges with right sides together taking a 1.5 cm (⅝ in) seam allowance. Clip the corners. Press the seams open. Turn the lining right side out.

5 Slip the case into the lining with wrong sides facing. Pin the gap on the lining around the zip. Slipstitch in place, see Hand Stitches. Turn the pencil case right side out.

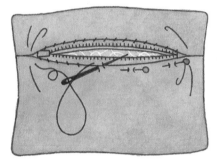

6 Slip the ribbon through the zip pull with the ends level. Stitch back and forth a few times across the ribbon 1.2 cm (½ in) from the zip pull. Trim the ribbon ends diagonally.

Rosette Cushion

Give a new lease of life to a plain cushion. Here, striped ribbons are gathered into rosettes and sewn in a grid formation to the cushion and topped with dainty buttons. It's fun to do and is a great opportunity to add a new accessory to your home with minimal outlay.

You will need
- Plain cushion
- 1 m 80 cm (2 yd) of 2.2 cm (¾ in)-wide striped ribbon
- Nine mother-of-pearl buttons, each 1 cm (⅜ in) diameter

1 Cut nine lengths of ribbon, each 20 cm (8 in). Press under 1 cm (⅜ in) at one end of each ribbon. Starting with a knot at the pressed end, sew a double length of sewing thread along one long edge of one ribbon with a running stitch. Pull up the stitches to gather the ribbon tightly into a rosette. Secure the shape with a few stitches at the centre. Repeat to make rosettes from the other ribbons.

2 Arrange the rosettes on the centre of the front of the cushion in three rows of three rosettes. Sew in place with a button on the centre of each rosette.

Trimmed Towel

Give a personal touch to a guest towel with bands of pretty ribbons, then take the idea a step further and add fabric flowers formed from rouleaux.

You will need
- Guest towel
- 3.8 cm (1½ in)-wide patterned ribbon, twice the width of the towel plus 4 cm (1½ in)
- 35 cm (14 in) square of pink striped fabric
- Two buttons each 6 mm (¼ in) diameter

Cutting out
- From pink striped fabric, cut two bias strips 42 x 3 cm (16½ x 1¼ in) for the rouleaux, see the Cutting Bias Strips technique on page 28.

1 Cut the length of ribbon in half. Press under 1 cm (⅜ in) at one end of each ribbon. If your towel has woven bands, pin the ribbons along the bands, matching the pressed end to one long edge of the towel. If your towel doesn't have woven bands, pin the ribbons to the towel 8 cm (3⅛ in) above the short edges, matching the pressed end to one long edge of the towel. Turn under the other end of the ribbons to match the other long edge of the towel. Slipstitch the ends of the ribbons to the towel. Follow the Applying Ribbons technique on page 36 to stitch the ribbons to the towel.

2 Make the rouleax following step 1–3 of the Making a Rouleau technique on page 34. Divide the rouleau into sixths, marking each division with a pin. Anchor a needle threaded with a double length of thread to one end. Fold the rouleaux at the first pin and insert the needle through the fold. Repeat at each pin position. Pull up the thread to form 'petals'. Sew the ends of the rouleau together to make the flower. Secure the shape with a few stitches at the centre. Arrange the flowers on the towel at one end of a ribbon. Sew in place then sew a button at the flower centres.

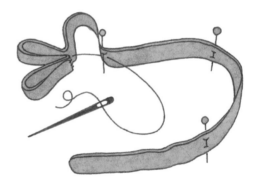

Crop Top

This short, funky top looks great layered over a longer top in the colder months or on its own in the summer. Just lengthen the pattern if you'd prefer a longer length. Only a small amount of fabric is needed so you could make a few in different colours.

You will need
- 50 cm (⅔ yd) of 140 cm (55 in)-wide cotton or acrylic jersey fabric

Cutting out
Refer to the diagram with the T-shirt Dress.
- For the Small size, make the pattern on a 44 x 32.5 cm (17⅜ x 12¾ in) rectangle of paper.
- For the Medium size, make the pattern on a 44 x 33.5 cm (17⅜ x 13 in) rectangle of paper.
- From cotton or acrylic jersey fabric, cut one pair of crop tops cut to the fold, cutting one crop top along the back neck and the other crop top along the front neck.

1 Set the sewing machine to a 2 mm (¹⁄₁₆ in)-wide zig-zag stitch; this will allow the seams to stretch when you wear the top but not to break the stitching. Use a ballpoint needle on jersey fabric. With right sides together, pin the tops together along the shoulders. Stitch the shoulder seams, taking a 1.5 cm (⅝ in) seam allowance and stopping 1.5 cm (⅝ in) to each side of the neck edge. Press the seam open.

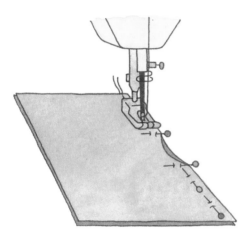

2 Press under 1.5 cm (⅝ in) on the neck and sleeve edges, neatly folding under the corners of the shoulders at the neck edge. Set the machine to a 5 mm (¼ in)-wide zig-zag stitch and stitch close to the raw edge of the neck and across the shoulder seams to hem the neck edge.

3 Open out the pressed edges of the sleeves at the side edges. Pin the side seams with right sides together. Set the sewing machine to a 2 mm (¹⁄₁₆ in)-wide zig-zag stitch again. Starting 1.5 cm (⅝ in) in from the sleeve edges, stitch the side seams, taking a 1.5 cm (⅝ in) seam allowance. To reinforce the seam, stitch the curve of the side seams again just inside the seams. Press the seams open, the curve of the seam will not lie completely flat so run the toe of the iron along the line of the seam. Refold the sleeve hems, folding under the corners neatly at the side seams.

4 Set the machine to a 5 mm (¼ in)-wide zig-zag stitch and stitch close to the raw edge of the sleeve edges to hem them. Follow the Making a Plain Hem technique on page 26 to press a 3 cm (1¼ in) deep hem on the lower edges. See the Herringbone Stitch technique on page 23 to sew the hem in place.

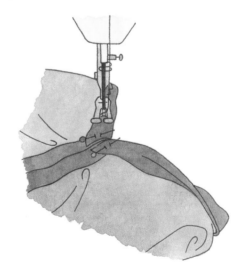

T-Shirt Dress

A T-shirt dress is a summer must-have. The shoulder edges on this neat version are caught together with a row of buttons and there are deep side slits so that you can boldly stride out. Make the dress from jersey fabric and stitch with a ballpoint needle.

You will need
- 1 m (1¼ yd) of 140 cm (55 in) wide striped cotton or acrylic jersey fabric
- 6 x 1.5 cm (⅝ in) diameter metal buttons

Cutting out
Refer to the diagram on the following pages.
For the Small size, make the pattern on a 90 x 32.5 cm (35½ x 12¾ in) rectangle of paper.
For the Medium size, make the pattern on a 90 x 33.5 cm (35½ x 13 in) rectangle of paper.
- From striped jersey fabric, making sure that the stripes are matched when you fold the fabric, cut one pair of T-shirt dresses to the fold, cutting one dress along the back neck and the other dress along the front neck. Cut the same colour stripe level with the lower edge on both dresses so that the stripes match when you join the side seams.

1 Pin the dresses together along the side edges with right sides facing and matching the stripes. Set the sewing machine to a 2 mm (¹⁄₁₆ in) wide zig-zag stitch. Starting 1.5 cm (⅝ in) from the sleeve edges, stitch the side seams to 25 cm (10 in) above the lower edge, taking a 1.5 cm (⅝ in) seam allowance. To reinforce the seam, stitch the curve of the side seams again just inside the seams. Press the seams open; the curve of the seam will not lie completely flat so run the toe of the iron along the line of the seam itself.

2 Press under 1.5 cm (⅝ in) on the sleeve edges, folding under the corners neatly at the side seams. Set the machine to a 5 mm (¼ in) wide zig-zag stitch and stitch close to the raw edges to hem the sleeve edges.

3 Next, press under 1.5 cm (⅝ in) on the shoulder then the neck edges, folding under the corners of the neck neatly. Press under 1.5 cm (⅝ in) on the lower edge. Use a 5 mm (¼ in) wide zig-zag stitch to stitch close to the raw edges to hem the shoulder, neck and lower edges.

4 Press under 1.5 cm (⅝ in) on the side edges below the side seams to form the slits. Use a 5 mm (¼ in) wide zig-zag stitch to stitch close to the raw edges and across the side seams to hem the slits.

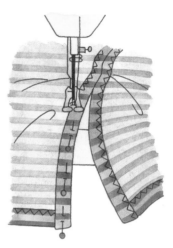

5 Turn the dress right side out and pin the shoulder edges together. Use a double length of sewing thread to catch the shoulders together at the neck edge. Oversew the edges for 6 mm (¼ in) then sew a button on top. Repeat to sew the shoulder edges together at 6.5 cm (2½ in) intervals with a button sewn on top.

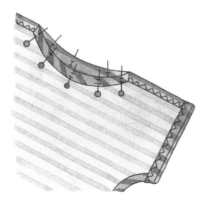

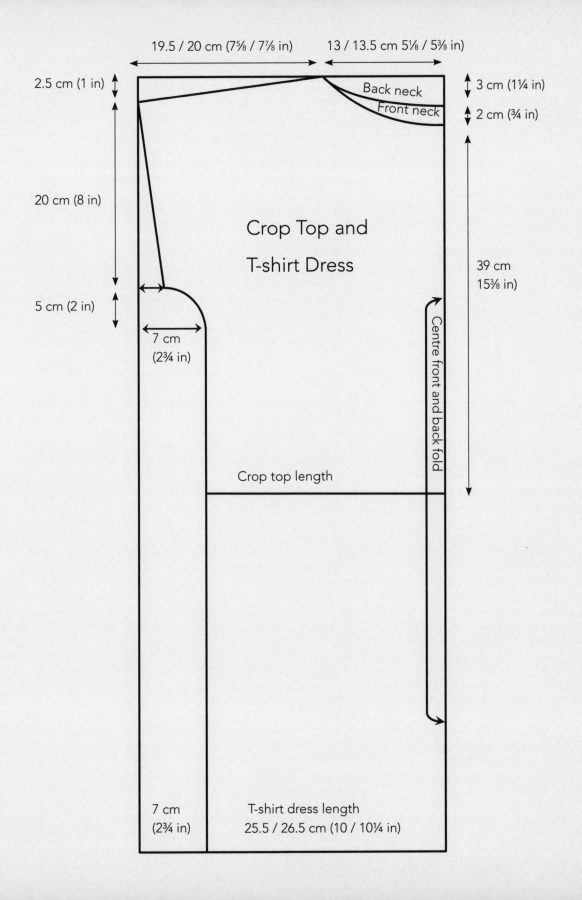

19.5 / 20 cm (7⅝ / 7⅞ in)

13 / 13.5 cm 5⅛ / 5⅜ in)

2.5 cm (1 in)

3 cm (1¼ in)

Back neck

Front neck

2 cm (¾ in)

20 cm (8 in)

Crop Top and

T-shirt Dress

39 cm

15⅜ in)

5 cm (2 in)

7 cm
(2¾ in)

Centre front and back fold

Crop top length

7 cm
(2¾ in)

T-shirt dress length
25.5 / 26.5 cm (10 / 10¼ in)

Circular Skirt

A circular skirt is a classic that is never out of fashion. This skirt fastens with a lapped zip for a sleek fit and for simplicity, the waist edge is discreetly finished with bias binding.

Tip... Pin the side seams of the skirt before stitching and try it on with the pins on the outside. Repin at the waist to adjust the fit if necessary. Use the new pinned position as the seam lines, have the seam allowance even on each side edge.

You will need
- 1.2 m (1½ yd) of 112 cm (44 in)-wide light blue/cream patterned cotton fabric
- One cream zip (zipper) 18 cm (7 in)
- 80 cm (1 yd) of 1.2 cm (½ in)-wide cream bias binding
- One hook and eye fastening (optional)

Cutting out
Refer to the Making A Circular Pattern technique on page 22 and the diagram on the following pages, for the Small size, make the pattern on a 53.5 cm (21⅛ in) square of paper.
For the Medium size, make the pattern on a 54.5 cm (21½ in) square of paper.
- From patterned cotton fabric, cut one pair of skirts to the fold.

1 Stitch the waist edges of each skirt taking a 1 cm (⅜ in) seam allowance; this is stay-stitching and will stop the curved edge from stretching. Tidy the side edges with a zig-zag stitch (see the Tidying Seams technique on page 25). Pin two skirts together along one side edge with right sides facing. Taking a 1.5 cm (⅝ in) seam allowance, stitch the side seam, starting 18.5 cm (7¼ in) below the waist edge. Press the seam open, also press under the 1.5cm (⅝ in) on the opening edges above the seam.

2 With right sides facing up, slip the zip under the right-hand pressed edge. Pin and tack (baste) the pressed edge close to the zip teeth with the slider 2 cm (¾ in) below the waist edge. With a zipper foot on your sewing machine, stitch as close as possible to the teeth. Lap the left-hand pressed edge over the stitched edge by 2 mm (¹⁄₁₂ in). Pin, then tack the pressed edge in place, then tack across the base of the zip.

3 Use a zipper foot to stitch the zip 9 mm (⁵⁄₁₆ in) in from the left-hand pressed edge, then across the base of the zipper. Now unpick the tacking. With right sides together, stitch the other side seam, taking a 1.5 cm (⅝ in) seam allowance. Press the seam open. Open the zip. Refer to the Binding a Straight Edge then Finishing Binding technique on page 30 to bind the waist edge, taking a 1 cm (⅜ in) seam allowance on the waist edge and turning under the binding so that it is not visible on the right side. If you wish, fasten the waist edge with a hook and eye above the zipper. Follow the Hemming a Curved Edge technique on page 27 to hem the skirt.

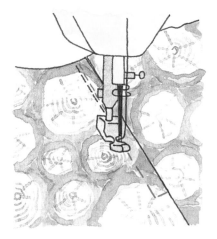

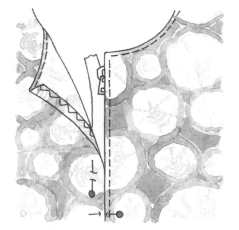

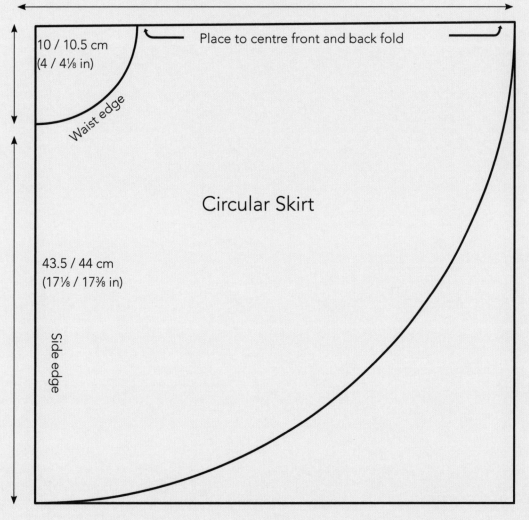

53.5 / 54.5 cm (21⅛ / 21½ in)

10 / 10.5 cm
(4 / 4⅛ in)

Waist edge

Place to centre front and back fold

Circular Skirt

43.5 / 44 cm
(17⅛ / 17⅜ in)

Side edge

Patchwork Scarf

This pretty scarf is just the thing to protect you from cool summer breezes. Choose floaty cotton fabrics such as voile or lawn, which are inexpensive and will drape well.

You will need

- 30 cm (⅓ yd) of three 112 cm (44 in) wide multi-patterned lightweight cotton fabrics
- 20 cm (¼ yd) of one 112 cm (44 in) wide multi-patterned lightweight cotton fabric
- 30 cm (⅓ yd) of pale grey pom-pom trim

Cutting out

- From four patterned fabrics cut eleven rectangles each 38 x 13 cm (15 x 5¼ in).

1 Pin the rectangles with right sides together along the long edges to make a long strip of assorted patterned fabrics. Stitch the long edges, taking a 1 cm (⅜ in) seam allowance. Press the seams open.

2 Fold the scarf lengthwise in half. Pin the raw edges together, matching the seams. Stitch the raw edges, taking a 1 cm (⅜ in) seam allowance and leaving a 10 cm (4 in) gap to turn the scarf right side out. Clip the corners then turn the scarf to the right side by pulling it through the gap. Press the scarf along the seam then press along the fold. Slipstitch the gap closed, see Hand Stitches.

3 Clip 18 pom-poms off a length of pom-pom trim. To finish, sew nine pom-poms equally spaced apart to each end of the scarf.

Sequinned Headband

Create some festival style with a delicately embellished headband. If you haven't tried beading before, sequins are a great introduction to the craft. They come in all sorts of shapes, sizes and colours, are widely available and cheap to buy.

You will need

- 70 x 10 cm (27 x 4 in) rectangle of lilac plain cotton fabric
- 70 x 10 cm (27 x 4 in) rectangle of lightweight iron-on interfacing
- 11 cm (4⅜ in) of 8 mm (⁵⁄₁₆ in) wide elastic
- 18 assorted pink, white, purple and light brown leaf-shaped sequins
- 5 g (¼ oz) of 4 mm (⅛ in) silver round sequins
- 5 mauve flower-shaped sequins
- 5 small silver-lined glass beads
- 5 g (¼ oz) of 4 mm (⅛ in) lilac round sequins

Cutting out

- Press interfacing to the wrong side of the fabric. From interfaced fabric cut a piece 60 x 6 cm (23⅝ x 2⅜ in) for the headband.

1 Press under 6 mm (¼ in) at the ends of the headband. Fold the headband lengthwise in half with right sides facing and pin the raw edges together. Stitch the long edge taking a 6 mm (¼ in) seam allowance. Turn the headband right side out with a bodkin then press the headband flat with the seam at the lower edge. Bring the pressed ends to meet. Slipstitch the pressed edges together.

2 Mark the underside of the headband with a pin 6.5 cm (2½ in) to each side of the join. Pin the ends of the elastic to the pinned marks. Now stretch the elastic to fit as you stitch close to the long edges and 1 cm (⅜ in) in from the ends of the elastic. Trim the ends of elastic just beyond the ends of the stitching. Starting at the centre of the headband, mark the right side with a pin at 5 cm (2 in) intervals, finishing before the ends of the elastic.

3 Use a single length of sewing thread and a fine crewel embroidery or a beading needle to sew the sequins and beads: Arrange two leaf sequins at one pinned mark. Sew the base of the leaves to the headband. Sew three silver round sequins at the base of the leaves. Sew two leaf sequins at the next pinned mark. Bring the needle and thread to the right side through one hole at the base of one leaf. Thread on a flower sequin and one silver-lined glass bead. Insert the needle back through the flower and leaf holes. Pull the thread to sit the bead on the centre of the flower. Repeat to alternate the beading sequence at all the pinned marks. Between the first and last beaded sequence, sew silver round sequins along the headband in a wavy row, then sew lilac round sequins along both edges of the headband.

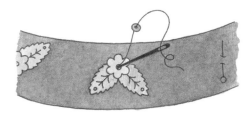

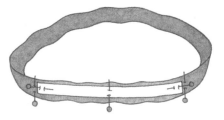

Aprons

Not just practical but smart too, these aprons have a roomy set of pockets and generous ties that are long enough to wrap around your waist and fasten at the front in classic Parisian waiter style. Choose a full or short apron, they make great gifts too.

You will need

- 70 x 25 cm (30 x 10 in) rectangle of olive green patterned cotton fabric for a full apron
- 70 x 25 cm (30 x 10 in) rectangle of light blue patterned cotton fabric for a short apron
- 80 x 75 cm (32 x 30 in) rectangle of light blue spotted cotton fabric for a full apron
- 70 x 60 cm (30 x 25 cm) olive green plain linen or cotton fabric for a short apron
- 2 m 90 cm (3⅓ yd) of 2.5 cm (1 in) wide white tape for a full apron
- 2 m 30 cm (2⅔ yd) of 2.5 cm (1 in) wide white tape for a short apron

Cutting out

- From patterned fabric, for each apron, cut a 67 x 22 cm (26½ x 8⅝ in) rectangle for the pocket.
- For the full apron, refer to the diagram on the following pages. The diagram is so simple that you can draw it directly onto your fabric without making a paper pattern. Cut a 76 x 67 cm (30 x 26½ in) rectangle of light blue spotted fabric. Fold the rectangle in half parallel with the long edges and pin the raw edges together. Follow the diagram to draw the slanted line. Cut along the slanted line. Unpin the apron and open it out.
- For the short apron, cut a 67 x 56 cm (26½ x 22 in) rectangle of olive green fabric.

1 Refer to the Making a Plain Hem technique on page 26 and press a 1.5 cm (⅝ in) deep hem on the long upper edge of the pocket. Stitch close to the inner pressed edge. Press under 1.5 cm (⅝ in) on the long lower edge of the pocket. With right sides facing up, pin the pocket to the apron with the lower pressed edge 18.5 cm (7¼ in) above the short lower edge of the full apron or long lower edge of the short apron.

2 Tack (baste) the side raw edges of the pocket and apron together. Stitch close to the lower pressed edge, then 6 mm (¼ in) inside the pressed edge. Divide the pocket in half and mark the division with a row of pins parallel with the side edges. Stitch the division, stitching back and forth a few times at the top of the pocket to reinforce the stitching. See the Making a Plain Hem technique on page 26 to make a 1.5 cm (⅝ in) deep hem on the raw edges of the apron, stitching close to the inner pressed edges.

3 Cut two 115 cm (48 in) long tapes for the ties. Cut one 60 cm (23½ in) long tape for the neck tape. Refer to the Stitching Ends technique on page 31 to stitch the tapes: stitch both ends of the neck tape 3.5 cm (1½ in) below the upper edge and just inside the corners of the upper edge of the full apron. Next, stitch the ties 3.5 cm (1½ in) in from the top of the side edges of the full apron. On the short apron, stitch the ties 3.5 cm (1½ in) below the upper edge and 3.5 cm (1½ in) in from the side edges. Cut the raw ends of the ties diagonally.

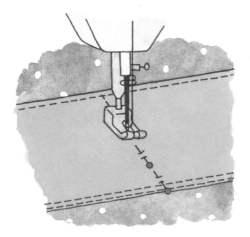

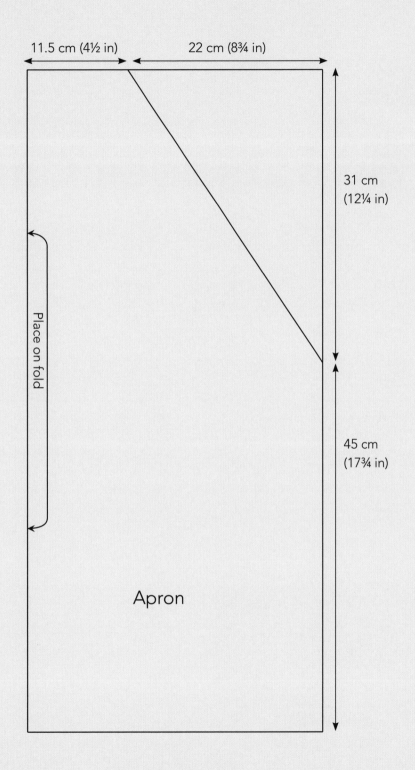

11.5 cm (4½ in)

22 cm (8¾ in)

31 cm (12¼ in)

45 cm (17¾ in)

Place on fold

Apron

Sunglasses Case

Generously sized for the most flamboyant pair of sunnies, this sunglasses case is padded with wadding to protect its contents and is trimmed with a row of ribbon pennants.

You will need
- 30 cm (⅓ yd) of 2.5 cm (1 in) wide turquoise ribbon
- 30 x 25 cm (12 x 10 in) rectangle of white / yellow patterned cotton fabric
- 30 x 25 cm (12 x 10 in) rectangle of 135 g (4 oz) wadding (batting)
- 30 x 25 cm (12 x 10 in) rectangle of white lightweight cotton fabric
- 30 x 25 cm (12 x 10 in) rectangle of turquoise cotton fabric
- 30 cm (⅓ yd) of 1.8 cm (¾ in) wide turquoise bias binding

Cutting out
- From each of the white / yellow patterned fabric, wadding, white lightweight fabric and turquoise fabric, cut two rectangles 19 x 13 cm (7½ x 5⅛ in) for the cases.

1 Cut three 10 cm (4 in) lengths of ribbon. Fold the ribbons diagonally to form pennant shapes, matching the folds to the long edges of the ribbon. Press the ribbons and pin the edges in place. Cut the ends of the ribbons level with the short upper edges of the pennants.

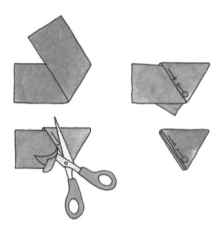

2 Pin the cut edges of the pennants in a row to the short upper edge of one patterned case on the right side, starting 1.2 cm (½ in) in from the long left-hand edge. Place the wadding right side up on the lightweight fabric then place the patterned fabric right side up on top. Smooth the layers and pin together; the lightweight fabric will protect your sewing machine from the wadding fibres.

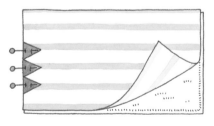

Tip... It is easier to stitch bias binding to the narrow opening of the case while the case is inside out.

3 Tack (baste) the outer edges together. Pin the cases together with right sides facing. Stitch the case, taking a 1.5 cm (⅝ in) seam allowance and leaving the short upper edge open. Carefully trim away the wadding in the seam allowance. Clip the corners and finger press the seams open, see step 2 of the Making a Filled Shape technique on page 36. Repeat to make the lining from the turquoise cases. Turn the lining right side out.

4 Slip the case into the lining matching the seams and raw edges. Tack the upper edges together. Follow the Binding a Circumference and Finishing Binding technique on pages 29 and 30 to bind the upper raw edges. Turn the case right side out.

Boxy Shoulder Bag

Simplicity is the key to this understated shoulder bag. It is a useful size and surprisingly roomy, measuring 25 x 20 cm (10 x 8 in) by 5 cm (2 in) deep. The bag is gently stiffened with heavy-weight sew-in interfacing which gives it shape yet is soft to handle. A wide webbing shoulder strap makes the bag comfortable to wear too.

You will need

- 30 cm (⅓ yd) of 137 cm (54 in) wide blue / cream patterned soft furnishing fabric
- 30 cm (⅓ yd) of 90 cm (36 in) wide heavy-weight sew-in interfacing
- 50 x 30 cm (20 x 12 in) rectangle of cream plain linen fabric
- 30 cm (⅓ yd) of 112 cm wide cream plain cotton fabric
- 80 cm (⅞ yd) of 5 cm (2 in) wide cream webbing

Cutting out

- From blue / cream patterned soft furnishing fabric and cream plain cotton fabric, cut two 27 x 22 cm (10⅝ x 8¾ in) rectangles for the front and back. Cut two 22 x 7 cm (8¾ x 2¾ in) rectangles for the side gussets. Cut one 27 x 7 cm (10⅝ x 2¾ in) rectangle for the base gusset.
- From heavy-weight sew-in interfacing, cut three 27 x 22 cm (10⅝ x 8¾ in) rectangles for the front, back and flap. Cut two 22 x 7 cm (8¾ x 2¾ in) rectangles for the side gussets. Cut one 27 x 7 cm (10⅝ x ¾ in) rectangle for the base gusset.
- From cream plain linen fabric, cut two 27 x 22 cm (10⅝ x 8¾ in) rectangles for the flap.

1 Pin the interfacing to the wrong side of the patterned fabric pieces and one cream flap. Tack (baste) the raw edges by machine or by hand. Taking a 1 cm (⅜ in) seam allowance, follow the Turning Gusset Corners technique on page 27 to stitch the patterned fabric side and base gussets to both short side and the lower long edge of the patterned fabric front and back. Turn the bag right side out.

2 Pin the flaps together with right sides facing. Taking a 1 cm (⅜ in) seam allowance, stitch the short side and long lower edges. Clip the corners then turn right side out. Press the flap and pin the raw edges together.

3 Pin each end of the webbing to the right side of the raw end of the side gussets of the bag. With right sides facing, pin the raw edge of the flap to the raw edge of the back bag. Tack the webbing and flap to the bag.

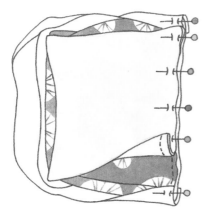

4 To make the lining from the cream fabric pieces, take a 1 cm (⅜ in) seam allowance and follow the Turning Gusset Corners technique as before to stitch the side and base gussets to both short side and the lower long edge of the front and back, leaving a 12 cm (4¾ in) gap in one side gusset seam to turn through. Slip the bag into the lining matching the seams, pin the upper raw edges together. Remove the bed of the sewing machine. Stitch the upper edges taking a 1cm (⅜ in) seam allowance.

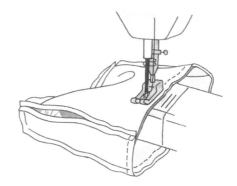

5 Turn the bag to the right side by pulling it through the gap in the lining. Slipstitch the gap closed (see Hand Stitches). Push the lining into the bag and press the upper edge. With the bed of the machine removed, topstitch the bag 7.5 mm (5⁄16 in) below the upper edge.

Handbag Mirror Case

If you are new to sewing, this pretty case for a handbag mirror is an ideal first project that you can then give as a thoughtful Mother's Day present. The case is custom made to fit any handbag mirror.

You will need

- Handbag mirror
- 25 x 20 cm (10 x 8 in) rectangle of magenta patterned cotton fabric
- 25 x 20 cm (10 x 8 in) rectangle of light pink cotton fabric
- 25 x 20 cm (10 x 8 in) rectangle of iron-on medium loft fleece
- 25 cm (⅓ yd) of co-ordinating ric-rac braid
- 25 cm (⅓ yd) of 6 mm (¼ in) wide Funny Road ribbon
- One 1.2 cm (½ in) white pearlised flower button

Cutting out

- Measure the height and width of the mirror. From patterned fabric, iron-on fleece and plain fabric, cut one rectangle that measures twice the height plus 3.5 cm (1⅜ in) x the width plus 2.5 cm (1 in).

1 Use a machine tacking (basting) stitch to sew a length of ric-rac braid to the right side of the patterned case 2 cm (¾ in) in from one side edge. Pin a length of ribbon on top, covering one edge of the ric-rac. Stitch close to both long edges of the ribbon, see the Applying Ribbon technique on page 36. Press the medium loft fleece to the wrong side of the patterned case. Pin the patterned and plain case together with right sides facing. Taking a 6 mm (¼ in) seam allowance, stitch the outer edges, leaving a 6 cm (2⅜ in) gap in one side edge to turn through. Clip the corners and turn right side out.

2 Press the outer edges, then slipstitch the gap closed (see Hand Stitches). With the patterned case facing outward, fold the case in half across its width. Pin the side edges together. Slipstitch the side edges securely together starting at the fold and finishing 2 cm (¾ in) below the upper edge, push the plain fabric to the inside as you stitch. Sew a flower button to the ribbon 2.5 cm (1 in) above the lower edge.

Bedroom Tidy

A humble clothes hanger provides the support for this neat storage design. A row of pockets can store jewellery and the sort of small accessories that easily go astray. Necklaces and bracelets can be hung around the hook and brooches pinned on. A row of mini pom-poms gives a cute finish to the tidy.

You will need
- Clothes hanger, 41 cm (16⅛ in) wide or narrower
- 40 cm (½ yd) of 137 cm (54 in) wide pink plain upholstery cotton fabric
- 50 x 20 cm (20 x 8 in) rectangle of pink patterned cotton fabric
- 50 cm (⅔ yd) of cream mini pom-pom trim

Cutting out
- From pink plain fabric, cut two 45.5 x 30 cm (18 x 12 in) rectangles for the tidy.
- From pink patterned fabric, cut one 45.5 x 17 cm (18 x 6¾ in) rectangle for the pocket.

1 Pin the tidies together. Place the clothes hanger on top with the upper edge of the hanger centred on the long upper edge of the tidy. Draw along the upper edge of the hanger with a sharp HB pencil, extending the lines to reach the short side edges of the tidy. Remove the hanger and cut along the drawn lines.

2 Follow the Making a Plain Hem technique on page 26 to press a 2 cm (¾ in) deep hem on the long upper edge of the pocket. Stitch close to the inner pressed edge. With right sides facing up and matching the lower raw edges, place the pocket on one tidy. Pin the lower edge. Next, pin the side edges, positioning the corners of the hemmed edges 6 mm (¼ in) inside the raw edges of the tidy. Tack the side and lower edges by machine or by hand.

3 With pins, divide the pocket into three equal sections parallel with the side edges of the tidy. Stitch along the divisions, stitching back and forth at the top of the pocket to reinforce the stitching.

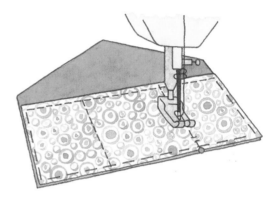

4 Press under 1.5 cm (⅝ in) on the lower edge of both tidies. Pin the tidies together with right sides facing. Take a 1.5 cm (⅝ in) seam allowance to stitch the side and sloping edges, leaving a 1.5 cm (⅝ in) gap at the centre of the sloping edges for the hook. Clip the corners, press the seam open then turn the tidy right side out.

5 Insert the hanger into the tidy and bring the hook to the outside through the gap. Pin mini pom-pom trim under the pressed edge of the pocket. Pin and tack the pressed edges together. Stitch close to the pressed edge then 6 mm (¼ in) inside it.

Jeans Gadget Bag

It's often a sad day when we must admit that a favourite pair of jeans are past their best. Don't despair, upcycle the jeans to make a couple of across-body bags — one pair of jeans will provide a bag for you and one for a friend, they are ideal to keep technical gadgets close at hand.

You will need

- Old pair of jeans
- Two 1.5 cm (⅝ in) metal eyelets and fixing tool
- 1 m 50 cm (1¾ yd) of 3 cm (1¾ in) wide striped ribbon

Cutting out

- From a pair of jeans, cut off the leg 18 cm (7 in) above the hem for one bag.

Tip... Don't use your skinniest jeans, the hem of the leg needs to have a circumference of at least 39 cm (15 ⅜ in).

1 Turn the leg inside out and fold along one seam. Pin and stitch the raw edges taking a 1 cm (⅜ in) seam allowance. Tidy the seam with a zig-zag stitch. Turn the bag right side out. Pin the front and back together along the hem. Follow the manufacturer's instructions to fix an eyelet through the front and back with the centre of the eyelets positioned 3 cm (1¼ in) below the hem and 3 cm (1¼ in) in from the side edges.

2 Press under 1 cm (⅜ in) at the ends of the ribbon. Mark the ribbon with a pin 14 cm (5½ in) in from the pressed ends. Thread each end of the ribbon through the front of the eyelets. Fold up the ends of the ribbon to match the pins. Pin the pressed ends in place to suspend the bag. Stitch close to the pressed ends then stitch 6 mm (¼in) in from the pressed ends.

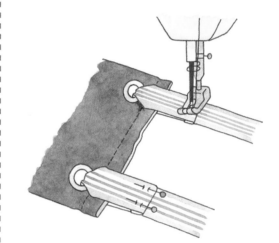

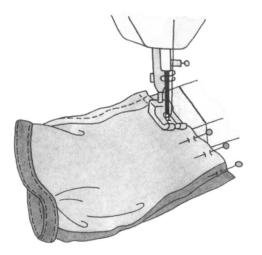

Upcycled Shirt

Give a plain shirt an edgy style by adding metal eyelets and studs. A row of eyelets on the sleeves allows you to fasten the sleeves at different levels and a few metals studs added to the collar will transform it.

You will need

- Long-sleeved shirt
- Six 8 mm (5/16 in) metal eyelets and fixing tool
- 80 cm (1 yd) of 2 cm (3/4 in) wide pink chevron ribbon
- 8–9 diamond-shaped metal studs
- Metal buttons, the same size and quantity as are already on the shirt

1 Fold the sleeves in half along the underarm seam. Mark the fold along the centre of the sleeves with a row of pins. On one sleeve, follow the manufacturer's instructions to fix an eyelet on the marked line 12 cm (4¾ in) below the end of the shoulder seam. Fix two more eyelets below the first at 7.5 cm (3 in) intervals. Repeat on the other sleeve. Roll up the sleeves. Cut two 40 cm (16 in) lengths of ribbon. Insert the ribbons through one set of eyelets and tie around the rolled sleeves. Cut the ribbon ends diagonally.

2 Arrange four studs on one corner of the collar. Hold one stud against the collar to press the studs through to the underside. Turn the collar over and place on a flat surface, press the prongs flat with the flat side of the closed blades of a pair of scissors. Repeat to fix studs to both corners of the collar. If the shirt has a pocket, fix a stud through the top edge, inserting the prongs through to the underside of the shirt, otherwise the weight of the stud will make the pocket droop. As a finishing touch, clip off the shirt's buttons and replace them with metal buttons, if you like.

Pillowcase

Pillowcases are very easy to make and are a simple way to add individual style to the bedroom. This spotty pillow case with its eclectic assortment of lace, ribbon and buttons will give a pretty vintage charm to your furnishings.

You will need

- 1 m 10 cm (1⅓ yd) of 112 cm (44 in) wide light blue spotted cotton fabric
- 60 cm (⅔ yd) of white edging lace
- 60 cm (⅔ yd) of 1.5 cm (⅝ in) wide patterned satin ribbon
- Four assorted buttons

Cutting out

- From light blue spotted fabric, cut one 78 x 53 cm (30¾ x 20⅞ in) rectangle for the front. Cut one 76 x 53 cm (30 x 20⅞ in) rectangle for the back. Cut one 53 x 24 cm (20⅞ x 9½ in) rectangle for the flap.

1 Pin the edging lace to the right side of the front with the decorative edge of the lace 13 cm (5⅛ in) in from one short edge. Pin patterned satin ribbon on top covering the straight edge of the lace. Follow the Applying Ribbon technique on page 36 to stitch the ribbon. Follow the Envelope Opening technique on page 30 to make the pillowcase. Sew buttons in a row along the edge of the ribbon starting 8 cm (3¼ in) below the upper edge.

Dipped Hem Skirt

Choose a soft, draping fabric such as Cupro or crêpe to make this elegant, unusual skirt. The skirt features an off-centre ribbon drawstring fastening. Choose the ribbon to co-ordinate with your outfit. When you have made the skirt, be bold and experiment by creating other versions with different shaped hems, perhaps asymmetrical or long at the back and short at the front.

You will need
- 1 m 20 cm (1½ yd) of 137 cm (54 in) wide plain pink Cupro or similar fabric
- 1 m 20 cm (1½ yd) of 4 cm (1½ in) wide navy double-faced satin ribbon

Cutting out
Refer to the diagram on the following page.

For the Small size, make the pattern on a 59 x 40.5 cm (23¼ x 16 in) rectangle of paper.

For the Medium size, make the pattern on a 60 x 41.5 cm (23⅝ x 16⅜ in) rectangle of paper.

- From plain fabric, cut two pairs of skirts.

1 Tidy the side, centre front and back edges with a zig-zag stitch, see the Tidying Seams technique page 25. Make two 1.5 cm (⅝ in) long vertical buttonholes 2 cm (¾ in) apart centrally on one skirt 8 cm (3⅛ in) below the upper edge.

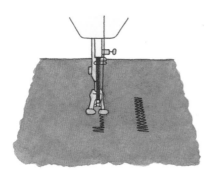

2 Pin the skirts together in pairs with right sides together. Stitch the centre front and back seams taking a 1.5 cm (⅝ in) seam allowance. With right sides facing, pin the skirts together along the side edges. Stitch the side seams taking a 1.5 cm (⅝ in) seam allowance. Press the seams open.

3 Refer to the Making a Casing technique on page 35 to make a casing on the upper edge.

4 Cut the ribbon in half. Fold one end of each ribbon over the ends of the elastic. Pin in place, then stitch across the ends taking a 1 cm (⅜ in) seam allowance. Turn the ribbons out to hide the seams. Fold the ribbon in half, then stitch across the ribbon 6 mm (¼ in) from the seams. Use a bodkin to thread the ribbon through the casing by inserting it through one buttonhole and

out of the other. When you wear the skirt, simply pull up the ribbon and fasten in a bow.

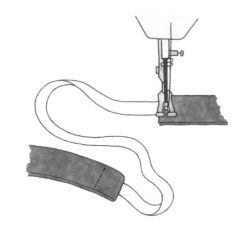

5 Start to fold under a 5 mm (⅛ in) hem on the lower edge. Stitch close to the fold using a long stitch on the sewing machine, folding under the hem as you stitch. Carefully trim away the raw edge close to the stitching. Fold under the hem along the new raw edge, stitch close to the inner folded edge.

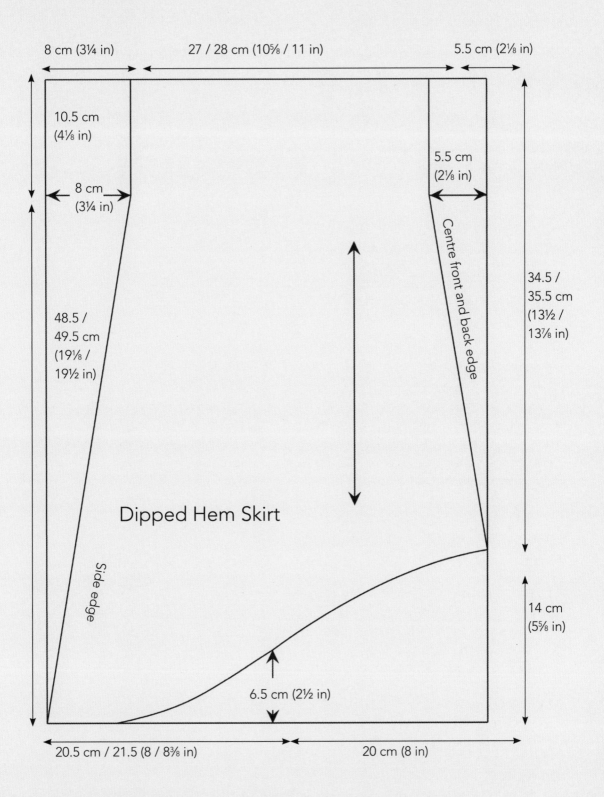

8 cm (3¼ in)

27 / 28 cm (10⅝ / 11 in)

5.5 cm (2⅛ in)

10.5 cm
(4⅛ in)

8 cm
(3¼ in)

5.5 cm
(2⅛ in)

34.5 /
35.5 cm
(13½ /
13⅞ in)

48.5 /
49.5 cm
(19⅛ /
19½ in)

Centre front and back edge

Dipped Hem Skirt

Side edge

14 cm
(5⅝ in)

6.5 cm (2½ in)

20.5 cm / 21.5 (8 / 8⅜ in)

20 cm (8 in)

Bird Brooch

Jazz up a jacket with this perky Scandinavian bird brooch. The bird is trimmed with beads and sequins and has a fancy set of tail feathers made from loops of cord and thonging.

You will need

- 10 cm (4 in) square of light green plain cotton fabric
- 10 cm (4 in) square of iron-on medium loft fleece
- 6 cm (2⅜ in) square of jade green plain linen fabric
- 2.5 cm (1 in) square of yellow plain cotton fabric
- 2.5 cm (1 in) square of lightweight iron-on interfacing
- Pale grey stranded cotton embroidery cotton
- Ten flat silver sequins
- One 3 mm (⅛ in) silver bead
- 10 g (½ oz) of tiny lime green beads
- 10 g (½ oz) of tiny jade green beads
- 10 cm (4 in) of pale grey rat's tail cord
- 10 cm (4 in) of jade green and aqua thonging
- Size 8 crewel embroidery needle
- Brooch pin

Cutting out

- From the light green fabric and iron-on medium loft fleece, cut one circle 8.5 cm (3⅛ in) diameter, for the bird.
- From the jade green fabric, cut one circle 4.5 cm (1¾ in) diameter, for the wing.
- Press the interfacing to the wrong side of the yellow square. From the interfaced square, cut one 1.7 cm (1¹⁄₁₆ in) square for the beak.

1 Press the fleece to the wrong side of the bird to fuse the layers together. With right sides facing up, pin the wing centrally to the bird, with the grain lines level. Thread a size 8 crewel needle with three strands of embroidery thread and knot the end. Blanket stitch the outer edge of the wing: Bring the needle out on the edge of the wing then insert it 3 mm (⅛ in) to the right-hand side and 3 mm (⅛ in) in from the edge. Bring the needle out on the edge of the wing, 3 mm (⅛ in) along from where it first emerged, keeping the thread under the needle. Pull the needle and thread through the fabric and continue all around the edge of the wing.

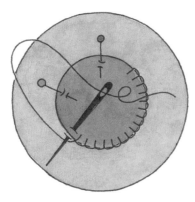

2 Press the beak diagonally in half with wrong sides facing. Fold the bird in half along the grain line and mark the fold with a pin at each end then open the bird out flat. Pin and tack (baste) the beak to the right side of the bird just below one pin, matching the raw edges. Carefully cut a 5 cm (2 in) long curved slit on one half of the bird just below the wing.

3 With right sides facing, fold the bird in half between the pins. Pin and stitch the outer raw edges together taking a 6 mm (¼ in) seam allowance. Clip the corners and the curves. Turn the bird right side out through the slit. Oversew the edges of the slit together. Press the bird.

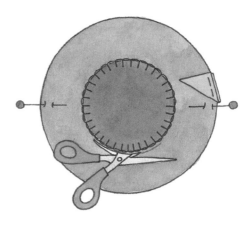

4 On the right side, sew a 3 mm (⅛ in) silver bead to the bird as an eye between the beak and wing. Sew tiny jade green beads around the eye. Use a single length of jade green sewing thread to sew seven silver sequins to the wing inside the blanket stitching. Sew seven tiny lime green beads close to the sequins. Fold the cord and thonging in half to form loops for the tail feathers and sew the ends together. Sew the ends of the tail feathers securely to the underside of the back of the bird. On the right side, sew three sequins to the bird in front of the tail feathers. Sew jade green beads along the curved edge of the bird. Sew a brooch pin to the underside of the bird.

Tote Bag

This classic tote bag is just the right size for a practical work bag — not too big and not too small. Use it to carry paperwork or fabrics, the tape measure patterned ribbon used here suggests keeping haberdashery inside.

You will need

- 70 x 50 cm (28 x 20 in) rectangle of aqua spotted soft furnishing cotton fabric
- 1 m 90 cm (2¼ yd) of 2.5 cm (1 in) wide patterned ribbon
- 90 cm (1 yd) of 1.5 cm (⅝ in) wide striped ribbon
- Sewing thread to co-ordinate with ribbons

Cutting out

- From aqua spotted soft furnishing fabric, cut two 40 x 33 cm (16 x 13 in) rectangles, one for the front and one for the back bag

1 Pin a 40 cm (16 in) length of patterned ribbon along the centre of the front bag on the right side parallel with the long side edges. Refer to the Applying Ribbon technique on page 30 to stitch the ribbon to the bag. Pin striped ribbon 6 mm (¼ in) to each side of the patterned ribbon and stitch in place.

2 Tidy the long side and short lower edges of the front and back with a zig-zag stitch, see the Tidying Seams technique page 25.

3 Cut two 70 cm (27 ½ in) lengths of patterned ribbon for the handles. Refer to the Stitching Ends technique on page 31 to pin and stitch the ends of the handles to the right side of the bags 10.5 cm (4⅛ in) below the short upper edge and 6.5 cm (2½ in) in from the long side edges.

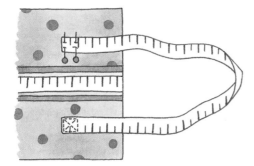

4 Pin the bags together with right sides facing. Stitch the side and lower edges taking a 1.5 cm (⅝ in) seam allowance. Press the seams open.

5 With right sides facing, pin the lower end of one side seam to match the end of the lower seam at the corner. Stitch at right angles across the seam 2.5 cm (1 in) from the corner. The seam will be 5 cm (2 in) long. Trim the seam allowance to 1 cm (⅜ in). Repeat at the other corner.

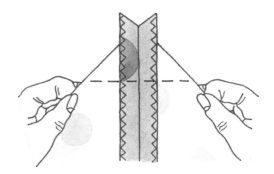

6 Neaten the seams with a zig-zag stitch. Refer to the Making a Plain Hem technique on page 26 to make a 2.5 cm (1 in) deep hem on the upper edge, stitching close to the inner pressed edge, take care not to catch in the handles.

Rose Hair Barrette

Once you have found how easy (and addictive) it is to make fabric roses, you may find yourself making them for all sorts of applications. Here, a trio of roses made from patterned fabrics and pair of fabric leaves are glued to a hair barrette (bobby pin).

You will need
- 60 cm (24 in) square of mid pink patterned cotton fabric
- 50 cm (20 in) square of light pink patterned cotton fabric
- 30 x 20 cm (12 x 8 in) rectangle of light green plain cotton fabric
- 8cm (3⅛ in) hair barrette (bobby pin)
- Strong textile glue

Cutting out
See page 28 for Cutting On The Bias.
- From mid pink patterned fabric, cut one 55 x 8 cm (21½ x 3⅛ in) strip, cut on the bias for the large rose.
- From light pink patterned fabric, cut two 50 x 6 cm (19½ x 2⅜ in) strips, cut on the bias for the small roses.
- From light green plain fabric, cut two 12 cm (4¾ in) diameter circles for the leaves. Cut one 10 x 5cm (4 x 2in) rectangle, on the bias for the base.

1 Fold the strips for the roses in half lengthwise with wrong sides facing. Pin the raw edges together, inserting the pins at right angles to the raw edges. Cut the raw ends in a curve. Keeping the raw edges level, start to coil the strip. Use a length of thread to catch in place just inside the raw edges with a few stitches. Sew a pleat in the raw edge about 6 mm (¼ in) deep. With the raw edges level and sewing through the layers from time to time, continue coiling and pleating the fabric until you reach the end of the strip, making the pleats deeper as you near the end of the strip.

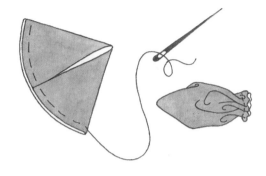

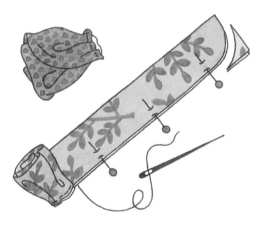

2 Press the leaves in half with wrong sides facing. Pin the ends of the pressed edges to meet on the circumference, matching the raw edges. With a length of thread, sew a running stitch 6 mm (¼ in) inside the raw edges, pull up the thread tightly to gather the fabric and secure in place.

3 With the raw edges level, pin each leaf to a small rose with the unfolded side of the leaf facing the rose. Sew together at the raw edges. Cut the corners of the base in a curve. Position the roses on the wrong side of the base with the large rose at the centre and the leaves on the small roses facing outwards. Pin in place by inserting pins through the base from the right side. Turn under the raw edges of the base and pin and slipstitch to the roses and leaves. Glue the base to the barrette (bobby pin) following the manufacturer's instructions.

Index